PILOT'S HANDBOOK

FLIGHT OPERATING INSTRUCTIONS
FOR
X-5 AIRPLANE

SERIAL NUMBER 50−1838
(MFG. MODEL DESIGNATION 60)

POWERED WITH TURBO−JET MODEL J35−A−17A ENGINE
$\left(\begin{array}{c}\text{ENGINE MFG. \& MODEL DESIGNATION}\\ \text{ALLISON 450−D4}\end{array}\right)$

MANUFACTURED BY
BELL AIRCRAFT CORPORATION

CONTRACT A F 33(038) − 3298   SPECIFICATION NO. 60-947-001

CLASSIFICATION CANCELLED
~~(OR CHANGED TO~~

BY AUTHORITY OF $\frac{1}{4}$ USAF Twx.
(INDIVIDUAL OR WRITTEN AUTHORITY)

BY _A.R.Malache_   4/11/58
(NAME & GRADE OF INDIVIDUAL MAKING CHANGE)   (DATE)

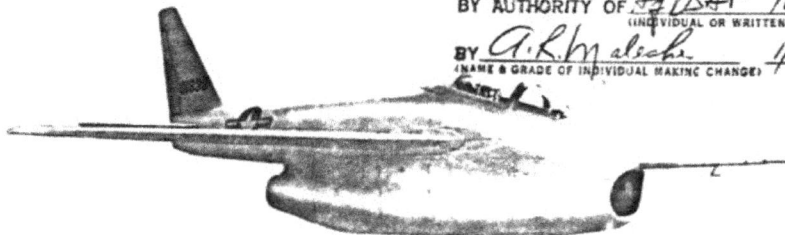

APPROVED BY CHIEF, ENG. DIV.

_____   _____
                                  MONTH − DAY − YEAR

Flight Operating Instructions
for
X-5 Airplane

©2009 PERISCOPE FILM LLC
ALL RIGHTS RESERVED
WWW.PERISCOPEFILM.COM

ISBN # 978-1-935327-69-1   1-935327-69-0

TABLE OF CONTENTS

ILLUSTRATIONS

INTRODUCTION

This handbook contains the information necessary to enable USAF personnel to operate the X-5 airplane, its equipment, and components. The handbook is divided into four sections and an appendix to facilitate easy comprehension. The handbook in its entirety covers the complete airplane; the various sections may be used for reference.

SECTION I - DESCRIPTION

The airplane, its equipment systems and components are described in this section.

SECTION II - NORMAL OPERATING INSTRUCTIONS

Instructions in the form of procedure steps, to complete a mission are contained in this section.

SECTION III - EMERGENCY OPERATING INSTRUCTIONS

This section contains instructions for meeting emergencies which might be expected to arise.

SECTION IV - OPERATIONAL EQUIPMENT

The operation of equipment and components of the airplane which are not essential for flight are contained in this section.

APPENDIX I - OPERATIONAL DATA

The limitations and charts for flight operation are contained in this section.

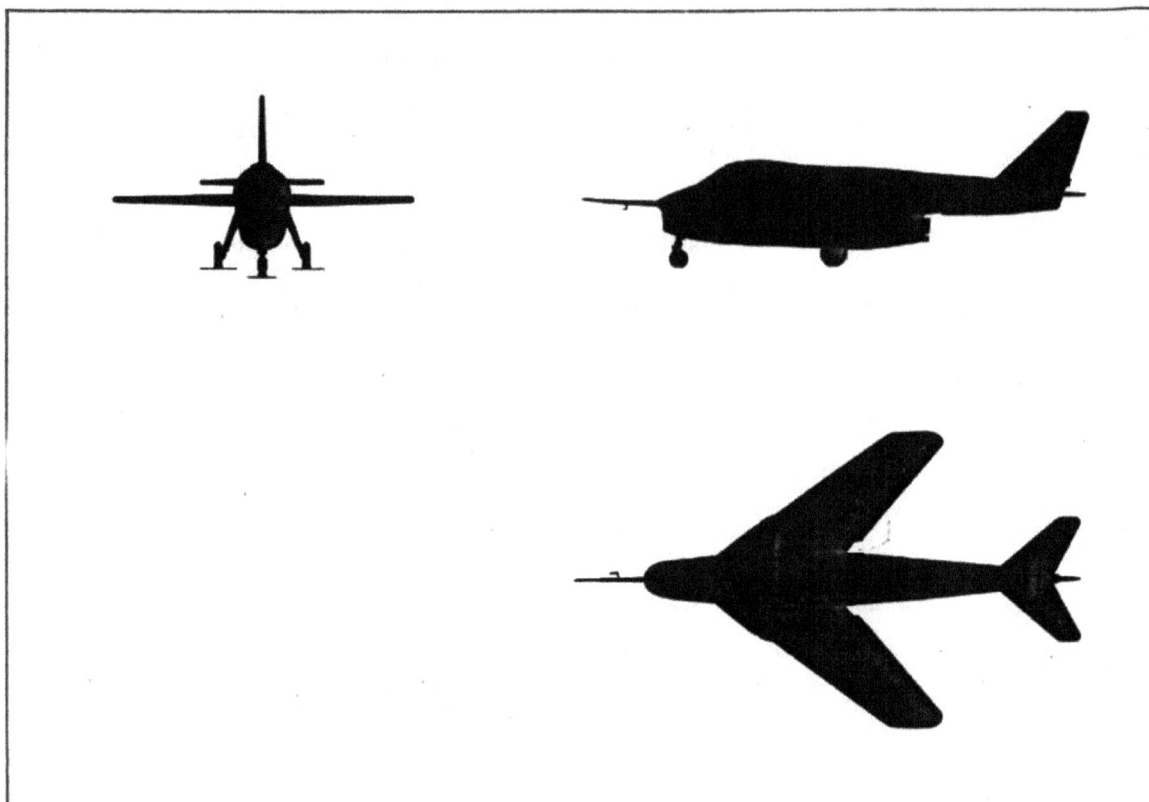

Figure 1-1. The Airplane

SECTION I

DESCRIPTION

1-1. THE AIRPLANE.

1-2. GENERAL.

1-3. The Bell X-5 airplane is a single-place, jet-propelled midwing monoplane, characterized by swept-back empennage and wings. The wings are adjustable from 20 degrees to 60 degrees in flight. The airplane is designed for high speed, high altitude, aerodynamic research. Power is supplied by a modified Allison J35-A-17A turbojet engine.

1-4. Over-all dimensions and gross weight:

Length	33 feet 6 in.
Height	12 feet 2 in.
Span (50° sweep)	23 feet 3.4 in.
Wheel base	12 feet 2 in.
Tread	6 feet 10 in.
Design gross weight	8980 pounds

1-5. POWER PLANT.

1-6. GENERAL.

1-7. The power plant is a modified Allison J35-A-17A turbojet engine, mounted within the fuselage, below and aft of the pilot.

1-8. POWER PLANT CONTROLS.

1-9. THROTTLE. The throttle (figure 1-2, reference 8) controls the amount of fuel supplied to the burners, thus regulating the speed of the engine. The microphone button (reference 7) is incorporated in the throttle handle, and a friction device (reference 10) is used to prevent the throttle from creeping during flight. The idle stop latch is operated to move the throttle into the "CUT-OFF" position. Throttle positions are: "OPEN", "IDLE" and "CUT-OFF". When the latch is operated and the throttle is moved to the full aft or "CUT-OFF" position, fuel flow to the burners is terminated. In the range from "IDLE" to "OPEN", fuel flow is increased or decreased as the throttle is moved fore or aft.

1-10. STARTER SWITCH. The starter switch (figure 1-3, reference 14) energizes the starter relay and ignition circuits when held in the "START" position. The relay remains energized until the starter has cranked the engine to approximately 23 per cent rpm, when it is automatically de-energized. In the event of a hot or false start, the relay may be de-energized by moving the switch to "STOP". The switch is spring-loaded to the center or off position.

1-11. STARTER — IGNITION TEST SWITCH. The starter and ignition system test switch (figure 1-3, reference 13) is spring-loaded to the center or off position. When held in "STARTER TEST" position, the starter relay is energized, but the ignition system

is not. When the switch is held in "IGNITION TEST", the ignition time delay relay is energized. The ignition test position can be used for making windmill starts above starter cranking speeds.

1-12. POWER PLANT INDICATORS. The power plant indicators consist of the engine tachometer, tail pipe temperature indicator and oil pressure gage (figure 1-4, references 10, 9 and 11).

1-13. OIL SYSTEM.

1-14. GENERAL.

1-15. The oil system consists of the oil tank mounted in the left side of the engine nacelle and adequate hoses and fittings. A sniffle valve in the vent line between the oil tank and the engine provides a slight amount of pressurization in the tank. Capacity of the system is three gallons, and it is serviced at the left side of the engine nacelle (figure 1-6, reference 8).

1-16. OIL SPECIFICATION. The oil used in this airplane shall conform to Specification No. MIL-O-6081.

1-17. OIL SYSTEM INDICATORS. The oil system indicator consists of the oil pressure gage mounted on the right side of the instrument panel (figure 1-4, reference 11). The instrument operates on a-c power supplied by the inverter.

1-18. FUEL SYSTEM.

1-19. GENERAL.

1-20. The fuel system consists of four interconnected cells which feed and vent as a single unit and are located within the fuselage aft of the pilot, two electrically driven submerged fuel pumps (one in number one cell, and one in number four cell), an electrically controlled shut-off valve, a main fuel control and pressure switch, an emergency fuel by-pass, a fuel strainer, and a fuel level transmitter and indicator. With the "SELECT EMERG" switch in "T. O. & LAND" position, the pressure switch operates the emergency fuel by-pass valve when the fuel pressure of the main fuel system drops below a preset value. A barometric combination vacuum and relief valve in the fuel tank vent line prevents fuel boil-off in a high-speed climb above 18,000 feet altitude. Below 18,000 feet the system is open-vented.

1-21. FUEL SPECIFICATION AND GRADE. The fuel used in this airplane shall conform to Specification MIL-F-5616, Grade JP-1, MIL-F-5624, Grade JP-3 or MIL-F-5572, Grade 100/130. The system is serviced at the top of the fuselage (figure 1-6, reference 5).

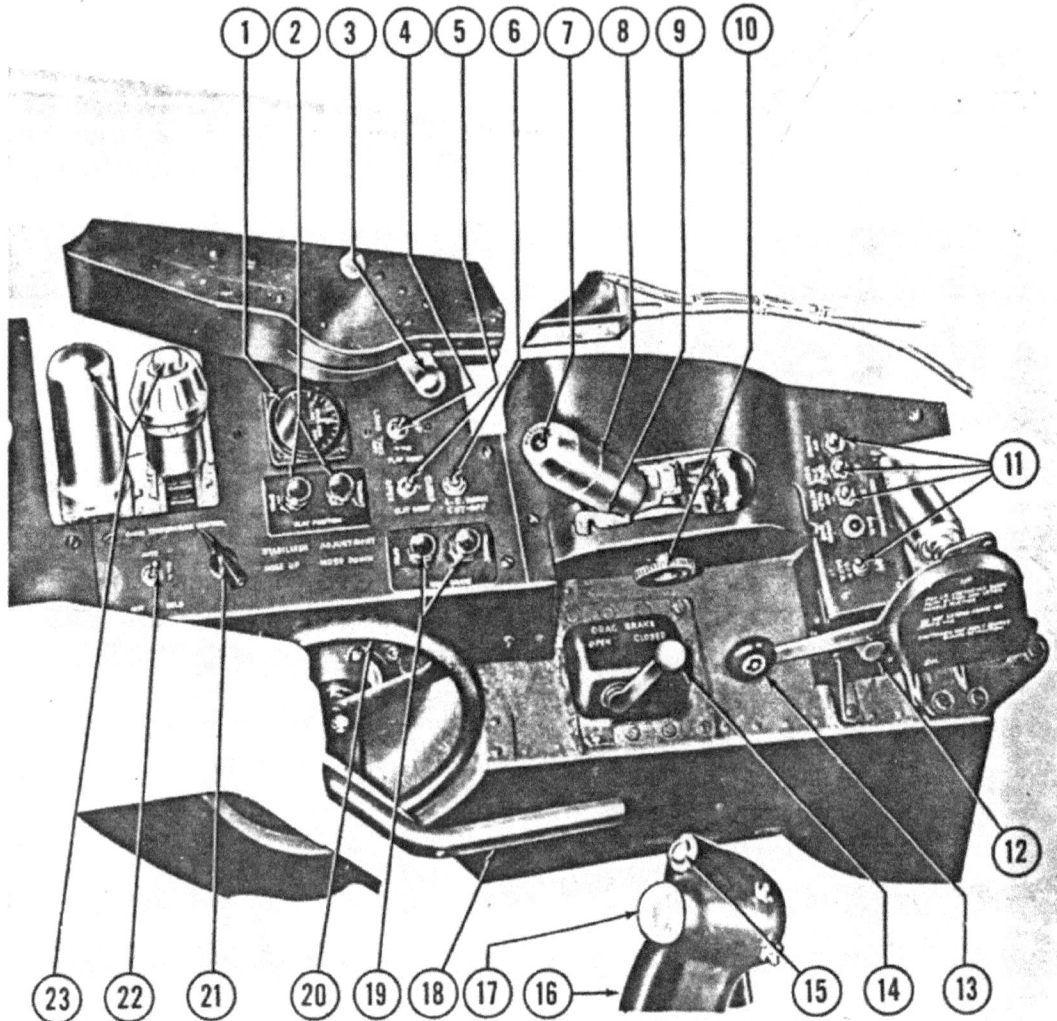

1. Stabilizer Position Indicator
2. Slat Position Indicator Lights
3. Cabin Pressure Dump Valve Control Lever
4. Flap Control Switch
5. Slat Control Switch
6. Landing Gear Warning Horn Cut Off Button
7. Microphone Button
8. Throttle
9. Latch
10. Throttle Friction Control Knob
11. Instrumentation Control Switches
12. Emergency Landing Gear Control Release Button

13. Landing Gear Control Lever
14. Drag Brake Control Lever
15. Wing Sweepback and Position Button
16. Control Stick
17. Stabilizer and Aileron Trim Control Button
18. Ejection Seat Handle
19. Drag Brake Indicator Lights
20. Stabilizer Trim Manual Control Wheel
21. Cabin Temperature Automatic Control Knob
22. Cabin Temperature Manual Control Switch
23. Anti-G Suit Regulator

Figure 1-2. Left Side View of Cabin

1. Canopy Control Crank
2. Canopy Locking Lever
3. Inverter Switch
4. Circuit Breaker Panel
5. Landing Gear Warning Horn
6. Channel Selector Switch
7. Radio Volume Control
8. Radio Switch
9. Radar Switch
10. Ejection Seat Handle
11. Emergency Fuel Control Switches
12. Fuel Shut-Off Switch
13. Starter and Ignition Test Switch
14. Starter Switch
15. No. 2 Fuel Pump Switch
16. No. 1 Fuel Pump Switch
17. Generator Switch
18. Battery Switch
19. Wing Sweep and Position Hand Crank

Figure 1-3. Right Side View of Cabin

RESTRICTED

Figure 1-4. Instrument Panel

1. Aircraft Altimeter
2. Airspeed Indicator
3. Fire Warning Light Test Switch
4. Fire Warning Lights
5. Directional Gyro
6. Fire Extinguisher Discharge Switch
7. Vertical Gyro
8. Turn and Bank Indicator
9. Tail Pipe Temperature Indicator
10. Engine Tachometer
11. Oil Pressure Gage
12. Fuel System Indicator Lights
13. Fuel Pressure Gage
14. Inverter Warning Light
15. Loadmeter (Ammeter)
16. Fuel Quantity Indicator
17. Voltmeter
18. Sweepback and Position Indicator

19. Oxygen Pressure Gage
20. Emergency Air Pressure Gage
21. Canopy Jettison Handle
22. Hydraulic Pressure Gage
23. Oxygen Blinker
24. Oxygen Regulator
25. Rudder Pedal Adjustment Locking Knob
26. Sweepback and Position Selector Panel
27. Clock
28. Flap Position Indicator
29. Accelerometer
30. "G" Unit Warning Light
31. Cabin Altimeter
32. Landing Gear Wheel Position Indicators
33. Landing Gear Warning Light
34. Machmeter
35. Compass

RESTRICTED

1-22. FUEL QUANTITY TABLE (U.S. GALS).

Tank No.	Usable Fuel	Expansion Space	Unusable Fuel Level Flight	Total Volume
	327.65	10.20	2.35	340.20

High speed level flight, fuel left in tank 2.35 gals.

1-23. NORMAL FUEL SYSTEM CONTROLS.

1-24. FUEL SHUT-OFF SWITCH. The "FUEL SHUT-OFF" switch (figure 1-3, reference 12) operates the electrically controlled fuel shut-off valve to establish or terminate fuel flow to the engine. When the switch is moved to "OFF", the valve is closed; moving the switch to "ON" opens the valve.

1-25. FUEL PUMP SWITCHES. The switches marked "FUEL PUMPS" (figure 1-3, references 15 and 16) control the two pumps submerged in the fuel tank. Switch "No. 1" controls the pump in the number one cell, and switch "No. 2" controls the pump in the number four cell. The pumps are energized when the switches are moved to "ON".

1-26. EMERGENCY FUEL SYSTEM CONTROLS.

1-27. EMERGENCY FUEL SELECTION SWITCH. The switch marked "SELECT EMERG" (figure 1-3, reference 11) has three positions: "T.O. & LAND", "START-NORMAL" and "FLIGHT EMERG". In the "START-NORMAL" position, normal fuel flow is established (see figure 1-5) and the red indicator light on the instrument panel (figure 1-4, reference 12) is lit. In the "T.O. & LAND" position, the green indicator light is lit, and the fuel control pressure switch is energized in a stand-by condition. If the fuel pressure drops below a pre-determined setting, the pressure switch closes, lighting the amber light on the instrument panel, opening the main fuel solenoid valve and closing the emergency fuel by-pass valve (see figure 1-5). In the "FLIGHT EMERG" position, the amber indicator light is lit, the main fuel solenoid valve is opened and the emergency fuel by-pass valve is closed, by-passing the main fuel control.

1-28. EMERGENCY FUEL CHECK SWITCH. The emergency fuel check switch (figure 1-3, reference 11) is spring-loaded in the "NORMAL" position. In this position, the emergency fuel system is controlled by the "SELECT EMERG" switch (reference 11). Moving the switch to "EMERG CHECK", with the "SELECT EMERG" switch in "START-NORMAL", will light the green indicator light and open the main fuel solenoid valve; the resultant drop in fuel pressure closes the fuel pressure control switch, lights the amber indicator light and energizes the emergency fuel by-pass valve. This is a ground check and must be made only with the "SELECT EMERG" switch in the "START-NORMAL" position.

1-29. FUEL SYSTEM INDICATORS. The fuel system indicators consist of the fuel quantity indicator (figure 1-4, reference 16), the fuel pressure gage (reference 13) and the three indicator lights. The green indicator light (reference 2) denotes the emergency fuel system is in a stand-by configuration; the red indicator light denotes the landing gear is down and "SELECT EMERG" switch is not at "T.O. & LAND"; the amber indicator light denotes emergency fuel system in operation.

1-30. ELECTRICAL SYSTEM.

1-31. GENERAL.

1-32. The electrical system is a single-wire, 24-volt d-c system, protected by manual reset circuit breakers mounted on the right console (figure 1-3). The combination starter-generator serves to charge the battery and operate the various electrical components after the engine is running. A voltage regulator controls the generator charging rate. An inverter to operate the gyro flight instruments and the wing sweep and position indicator circuits is connected to the d-c circuit.

1-33. EXTERNAL POWER RECEPTACLES. Two external power receptacles (figure 1-6, reference 9) in the right side of the engine nacelle are used when starting the engine or checking the electrical system of the airplane. When external power is used, the "BATTERY" switch (figure 1-3, reference 18) must be "OFF" to prevent by-passing the external power to the battery.

1-34. ELECTRICAL SYSTEM CONTROLS.

1-35. BATTERY SWITCH. The "ON-OFF" battery switch (figure 1-3, reference 18) disconnects the battery from the electrical system when moved to the "OFF" position.

1-36. GENERATOR SWITCH. The "ON-OFF" generator switch (figure 1-3, reference 17) grounds out the generator circuit when moved to the "OFF" position to facilitate radio noise level or electrical system checks. A guard over the switch excludes the possibility of inadvertently moving the switch to "OFF".

1-37. INVERTER SWITCH. The inverter switch on the circuit breaker panel (figure 1-3, reference 3) turns the inverter on to operate the gyro flight instruments when moved to the "INVER ON" position.

1-38. ELECTRICAL SYSTEM INDICATORS.

1-39. The d-c electrical system indicators consist of the voltmeter (figure 1-4, reference 17) and the ammeter (reference 15). The voltmeter registers the voltage of the electrical system. With the battery and generator switch "ON", after engine rpm has been increased above generator cut-in rpm, the voltmeter registers operating voltage. The ammeter (reference 15) registers the electrical load imposed on the system. The inverter warning light lights when the inverter is inoperative.

1-40. FLIGHT CONTROL SYSTEM.

1-41. GENERAL.

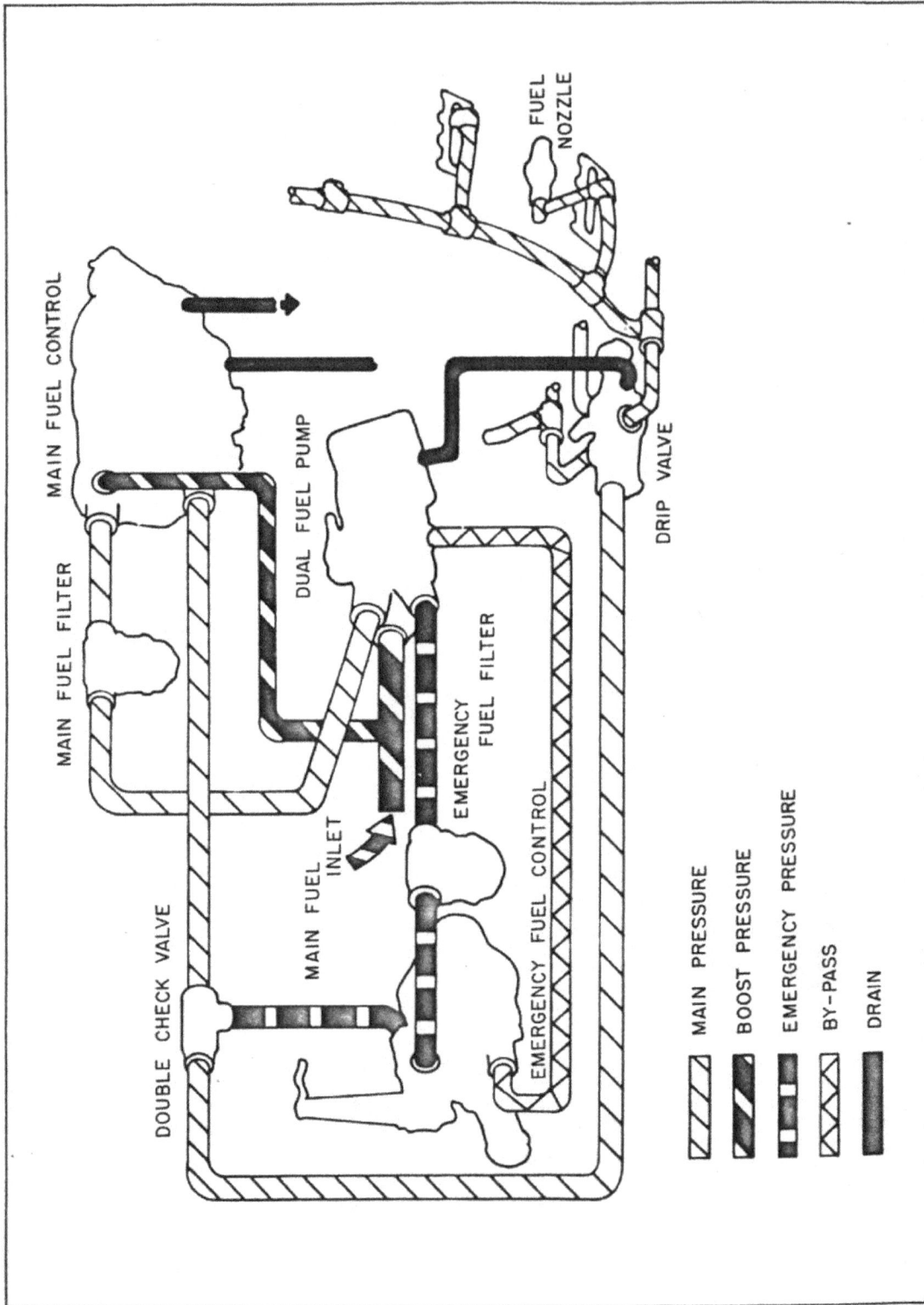

Figure 1-5. Fuel System Diagram

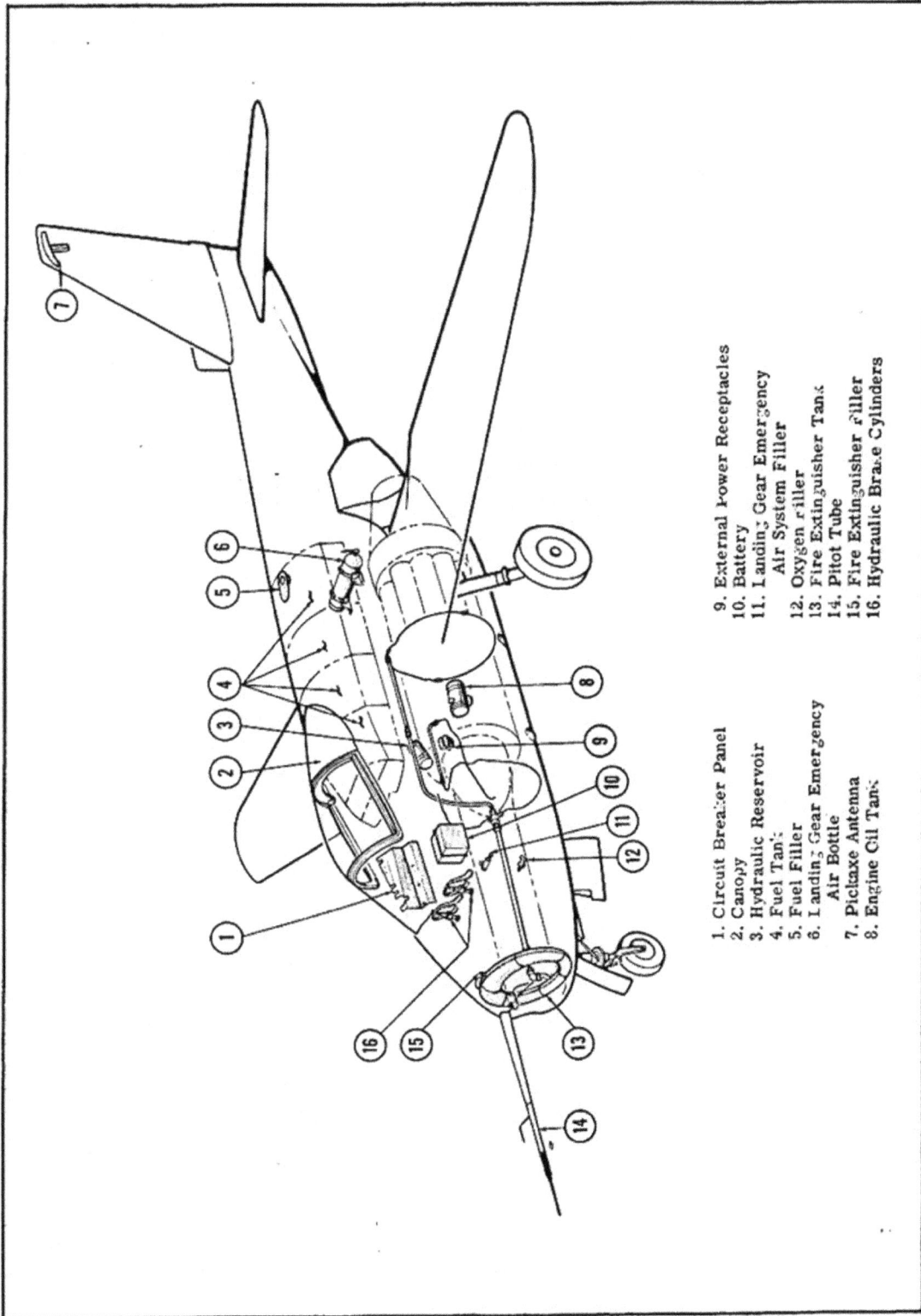

1. Circuit Breaker Panel
2. Canopy
3. Hydraulic Reservoir
4. Fuel Tank
5. Fuel Filler
6. Landing Gear Emergency
   Air Bottle
7. Pictaxe Antenna
8. Engine Oil Tank

9. External Power Receptacles
10. Battery
11. Landing Gear Emergency
    Air System Filler
12. Oxygen Filler
13. Fire Extinguisher Tank
14. Pitot Tube
15. Fire Extinguisher Filler
16. Hydraulic Brake Cylinders

Figure 1-3. General Arrangement Diagram

1-42. The flight controls include the control stick, the wing position and sweepback control (figure 1-4, reference 26), the rudder bar, flap control switch and slat control switch, the drag brake control lever, and the stabilizer and aileron trim switch.

1-43. CONTROL STICK. The control stick (figure 1-2, reference 16) operates the ailerons and elevators in the conventional manner. However, the stick grip incorporates the stabilizer trim and aileron trim control button (reference 17) and the wing position and sweepback control button (reference 15).

1-44. WING SWEEPBACK AND POSITION CONTROL. The wing sweepback and position control (figure 1-7), is connected to the actuating mechanism in the center section by selsyns and potentiometers in such a manner that the selection made with the pointer on the scales will be transferred to the mechanism, which will sweep the wings to within 1/4 degree and position the center section to within 1/5 inch of the readings on the indicator panel. Moving the pointer knob to the desired sweepback selection will simultaneously set the center section position, and both positions will be reached when the control stick button is pressed. To compensate for cp and cg changes, the center section may be moved fore or aft four and one-half inches, without changing the sweepback angle of the wings, by moving the position selection knob and pressing the button on the control stick grip. Total available travel of the center section is 27 inches, including synchronized and individual adjustment. Therefore, the travel is limited in the following configurations: at a 20 degree sweepback, aft travel is zero, forward travel is four and one-half inches; at 60 degree sweepback, forward travel is zero, aft travel is four and one-half inches. (See figure 1-8). Normal wing dihedral is zero throughout sweep.

1-45. RUDDER BAR. The rudder bar is installed in lieu of the conventional pedal installation. The toe plates are adjustable for leg length by pulling the knob (figure 1-4, reference 25) on the instrument panel. A fixed rudder trim tab is ground adjustable.

1-46. FLAP CONTROL SWITCH. The flaps are controlled by the switch marked "FLAP CONT" on the left console (figure 1-2, reference 4). The switch has four positions: "TAKE OFF", "LAND", "UP" and "OFF". When the switch is moved to "TAKE-OFF", the flaps move 20 degrees down; at "LAND" the flaps move 56 degrees down; at "UP" the flaps move fully up; in "OFF" the flaps maintain their position. The flap position is shown on the flap position indicator on the instrument panel.

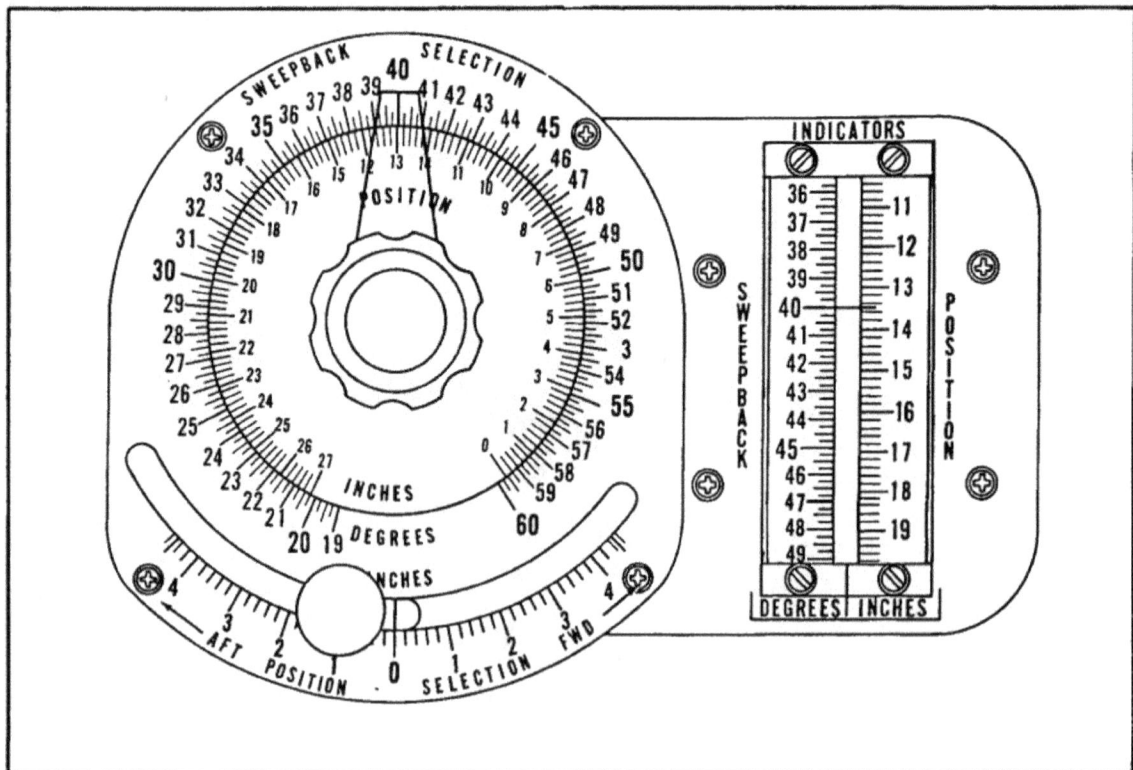

Figure 1-7. Wing Sweepback and Position Control and Indicator Panel

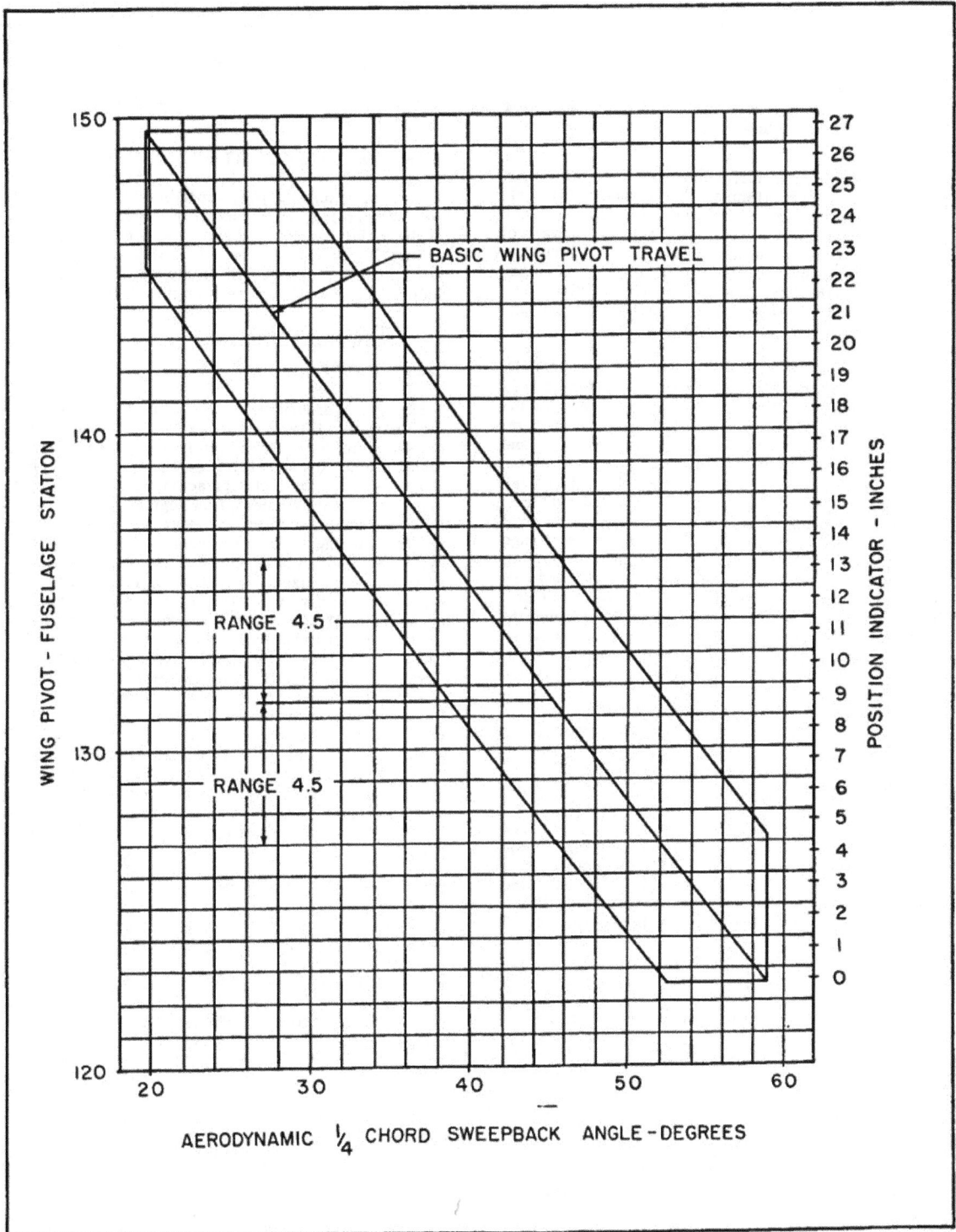

Figure 1-8. Wing Pivot Travel and M.A.C. Length Variation with Sweepback Angle

1-47. SLAT CONTROL SWITCH. The slats are controlled by the switch marked "SLAT CONT", on the left console (figure 1-2, reference 5). When the switch is moved to "OPEN" the slats move forward 10 per cent of the chord and downward five per cent of the chord. When the switch is moved to "CLOSED", the slats are closed and locked to the wing.

1-48. DRAG BRAKE CONTROL LEVER. The drag brake control lever (figure 1-2, reference 14) controls the hydraulically operated drag brakes on each side of the fuselage, below the wings and forward of the engine section. When the lever is moved to "CLOSED", the brakes are locked against the fuselage. When the lever is moved to "OPEN", the brakes extend. Flow regulators in the system assure uniform extension and retraction.

1-49. STABILIZER AND AILERON TRIM SWITCH. The switch on the top of the control stick (figure 1-2, reference 17), when operated laterally, energizes the actuator of the left aileron trim tab for lateral trim, i. e., pressing the switch left will trim the airplane left wing low; pressing the switch right, will raise the left wing. A ground adjustable trim tab is incorporated in the right aileron. Longitudinal trim is obtained by use of the manual override control wheel (figure 1-2, reference 20). In flight, a change in longitudinal trim may be accomplished by moving the switch fore or aft. Moving the switch forward will nose the ship down by energizing the adjustable stabilizer actuator in lieu of the elevators. Moving the switch aft will nose the ship up. Angular movement is five degrees up and eight degrees down. Stabilizer position is read on the indicator (reference 1) on the left console.

1-50. FLIGHT CONTROL SYSTEM INDICATORS.

1-51. WING SWEEPBACK AND POSITION INDICATORS.

1-52. The wing sweepback and position indicators are the card-type dials adjacent to the wing sweepback and position control. (See figure 1-4, reference 18, and figure 1-7). The "SWEEPBACK" indicator reads the degrees of wing sweepback, and the "POSITION" indicator reads the position of the center section in inches.

1-53. FLAP POSITION INDICATOR.

1-54. The flap position indicator (figure 1-4, reference 28) registers the position of the flaps when the "FLAP CONT" switch (figure 1-2, reference 4) is actuated.

1-55. SLAT POSITION INDICATOR LIGHTS.

1-56. The indicator lights on the left console marked "SLAT POSITION" (figure 1-2, reference 2) denote the position of the slats. When the slats are open, the "OPEN" indicator light is lit. When the slats are closed, both lights will be out. When the slats are in transit the amber light will be lit.

1-57. DRAG BRAKE INDICATOR LIGHTS.

1-58. The indicator lights on the left console marked "DRAG BRAKE" (figure 1-2, reference 19) denote the position of the drag brakes when the control lever (reference 14) is actuated. When the brakes are open, the "OPEN" light is lit. When they are closed, both lights will be out. When the brakes are in transit, the amber light will be lit.

1-59. STABILIZER POSITION INDICATOR.

1-60. The stabilizer position indicator on the left console (figure 1-2, reference 1) registers the position of the stabilizer. When the manual control wheel (reference 20) is rotated, or the switch on the control stick grip (reference 17) is moved fore or aft, the indicator will register the change in degrees of travel.

1-61. HYDRAULIC SYSTEM.

1-62. GENERAL.

1-63. The hydraulic system (figure 1-9) consists of the reservoir, filters, a variable displacement engine-driven pump, a pressure relief valve, drag brake and landing gear two-position selector valves, nose-wheel landing gear and door actuating cylinders, drag brake actuating cylinders, flow regulators, main wheel landing gear and door actuating cylinders, shuttle valves, landing gear main wheel down-lock release cylinders, and quick-disconnect fittings. The reservoir is pressurized from the engine compressor through a relief valve and an air filter at a maximum pressure of 12 psi. Hydraulic pressure is applied to the landing gear actuating cylinders when the control lever (figure 1-2, reference 13) is moved fore or aft. During retraction sequence valves transfer the hydraulic pressure from the landing gear cylinders to the door cylinders after the gear has reached the up limit. Hydraulic pressure is applied to the drag brake actuating cylinders by operating the control lever (figure 1-2, reference 14). Flow regulators in the system assure synchronized extension and retraction. Reservoir capacity is 1.6 U.S. gallons; system capacity is two U.S. gallons. Operating pressure is 2700-3000 psi.

1-64. OIL SPECIFICATION.

1-65. The oil used in this hydraulic system shall conform to Specification No. MIL-O-5606.

1-66. HYDRAULIC SYSTEM CONTROLS.

1-67. LANDING GEAR CONTROL LEVER. The landing gear control lever (figure 1-2, reference 13) operates the two-position valve to direct hydraulic pressure to the gear actuators. When the handle is moved to "UP", the down-locks are unlocked and pressure is applied to the retracting side of the actuator. When moved to "DOWN", the up-locks are unlocked and pressure is applied to the extension side of the actuators.

1-68. DRAG BRAKE CONTROL LEVER. The drag brake control lever (figure 1-2, reference 14) operates the two-position valve to direct hydraulic pressure to the drag brake actuators. Positions are "OPEN" and "CLOSED".

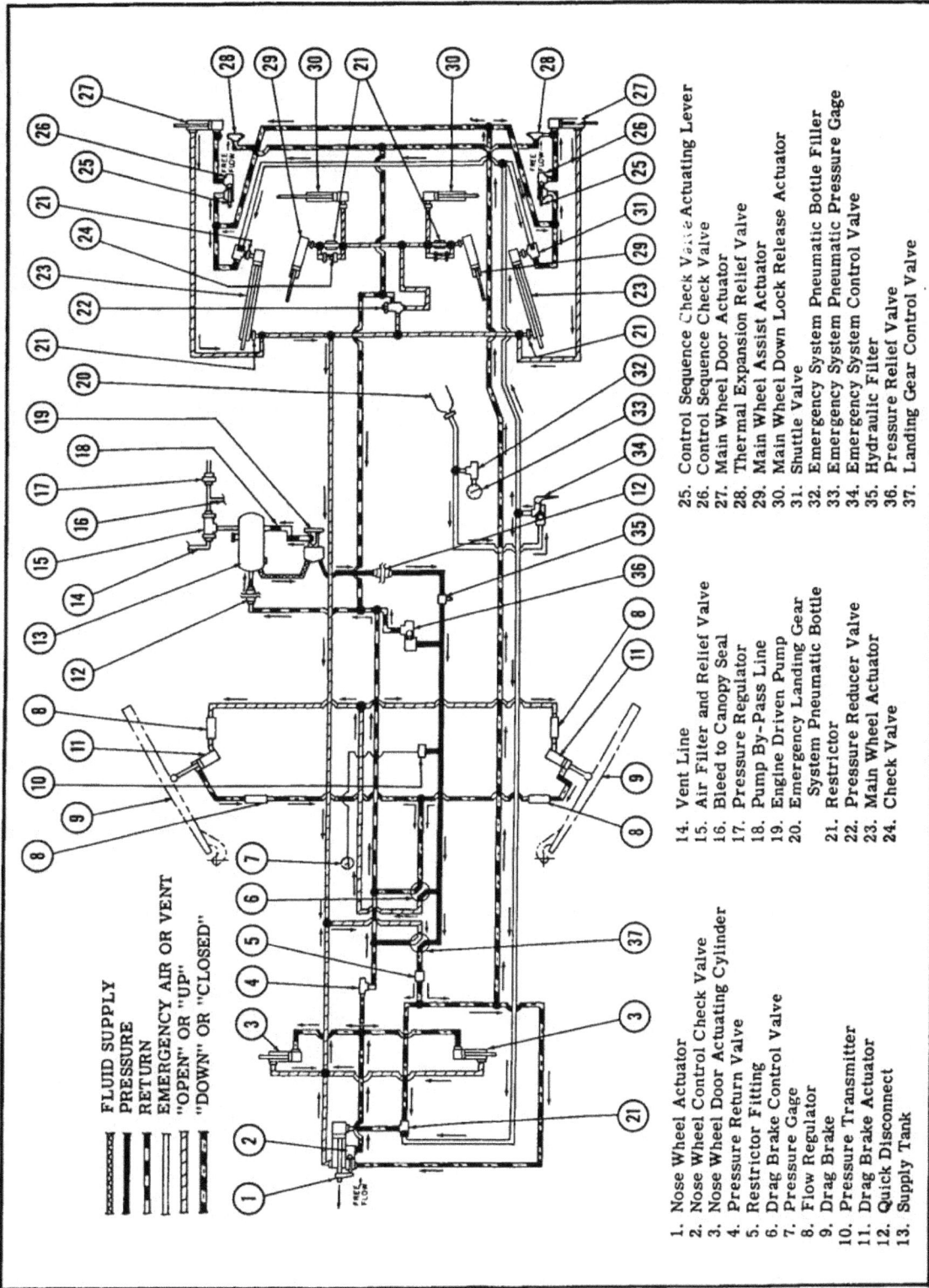

Figure 1-9. Hydraulic System Diagram

KEY:
- FLUID SUPPLY
- PRESSURE
- RETURN
- EMERGENCY AIR OR VENT
- "OPEN" OR "UP"
- "DOWN" OR "CLOSED"

1. Nose Wheel Actuator
2. Nose Wheel Control Check Valve
3. Nose Wheel Door Actuating Cylinder
4. Pressure Return Valve
5. Restrictor Fitting
6. Drag Brake Control Valve
7. Pressure Gage
8. Flow Regulator
9. Drag Brake
10. Pressure Transmitter
11. Drag Brake Actuator
12. Quick Disconnect
13. Supply Tank
14. Vent Line
15. Air Filter and Relief Valve
16. Bleed to Canopy Seal
17. Pressure Regulator
18. Pump By-Pass Line
19. Engine Driven Pump
20. Emergency Landing Gear
    System Pneumatic Bottle
21. Restrictor
22. Pressure Reducer Valve
23. Main Wheel Actuator
24. Check Valve
25. Control Sequence Check Valve Actuating Lever
26. Control Sequence Check Valve
27. Main Wheel Door Actuator
28. Thermal Expansion Relief Valve
29. Main Wheel Assist Actuator
30. Main Wheel Down Lock Release Actuator
31. Shuttle Valve
32. Emergency System Pneumatic Bottle Filler
33. Emergency System Pneumatic Pressure Gage
34. Emergency System Control Valve
35. Hydraulic Filter
36. Pressure Relief Valve
37. Landing Gear Control Valve

1-69. HYDRAULIC SYSTEM INDICATORS.

1-70. HYDRAULIC PRESSURE GAGE. The hydraulic pressure gage on the auxiliary panel (figure 1-4, reference 22) registers the system pressure.

1-71. LANDING GEAR SYSTEM.

1-72. GENERAL.

1-73. The hydraulically operated tricycle landing gear consists of the two main wheels and struts and the nose wheel and strut. The nose wheel is capable of swiveling 360 degrees to facilitate ground handling and taxiing. Hydraulic brakes in each main wheel are operated by toe plates on the rudder bar. The wheels retract aft into wells in the fuselage, and the hydraulically operated doors close and lock after the gear is fully retracted. The pneumatic emergency extension system is charged on the ground in accordance with the chart adjacent to the filler fitting. In the event of hydraulic system failure, the pneumatic system pressure can be applied to the down-side of the landing gear actuators through the shuttle valves, thereby extending the gear. (See figure 1-9.)

1-74. LANDING GEAR SYSTEM CONTROLS.

1-75. LANDING GEAR CONTROL LEVER. (Refer to paragraph 1-67.)

1-76. EMERGENCY LANDING GEAR CONTROL RELEASE BUTTON.

1-77. The emergency landing gear control down release button (figure 1-2, reference 12) permits the landing gear lever to be moved to a position at which the pneumatic control valve will extend the landing gear in the event of hydraulic failure. The emergency stop is held in and the lever is moved beyond the stop to actuate the pneumatic valve.

1-78. LANDING GEAR SYSTEM INDICATORS.

1-79. HYDRAULIC PRESSURE GAGE.

1-80. The hydraulic pressure gage (figure 1-4, reference 22) on the auxiliary panel indicates the operating pressure of the system.

1-81. EMERGENCY AIR PRESSURE GAGE.

1-82. The emergency air pressure gage (figure 1-4, reference 20) on the auxiliary panel indicates the pneumatic pressure in the emergency landing gear extension system.

1-83. WHEEL POSITION INDICATORS.

1-84. Three wheel position indicators (figure 1-4, reference 32) on the instrument panel show the position of each individual landing gear wheel. The red warning light (reference 33) indicates the gear is in transit or in an unsafe landing condition. The light also indicates the gear is not locked up and/or the doors are not closed.

1-85. WARNING HORN.

1-86. The landing gear warning horn (figure 1-3, reference 5) on the right console will sound if the throttle is retarded below minimum cruising rpm and the landing gear is retracted. A cut-off switch (reference 6, figure 1-2) shuts the horn off when pressed.

1-87. ENGINE FIRE DETECTION AND EXTINGUISHER SYSTEMS.

1-88. GENERAL.

1-89. Two separate fire detection circuits are installed in the fuselage, one in the engine accessory section, and another in the tail pipe section. The left red warning light (figure 1-4, reference 4) is connected to the engine accessory circuit, and the right red warning light (reference 4) is connected to the aft circuit. The test switch (reference 3) is actuated to test the circuits. The fire extinguisher is discharged into the engine nacelle when the "DISCHARGE" switch (reference 6) is actuated. A guard over the switch prevents inadvertent discharge.

1-90. CANOPY.

1-91. GENERAL.

1-92. The transparent bubble-type canopy slides up and aft on rails in the fuselage and on the canopy frame. When the canopy is closed, a pressure seal, inflated by a bleed-off from the hydraulic reservoir pressure system, prevents loss of cabin pressurization.

1-93. CONTROLS. The canopy is opened or closed by rotating the crank (figure 1-3, reference 1) above the right console. The canopy is opened from the outside by operating the crank in the fitting on the right side of the fuselage. The canopy is jettisoned in flight by pulling the canopy emergency release handle on the auxiliary panel (figure 1-4, reference 21).

1-94. EJECTION SEAT.

1-95. GENERAL.

1-96. An ejection seat which will catapult the pilot clear of the tail surfaces makes bail-out safe (figure 1-10). A type M-1 catapult attached to the back of the seat furnishes the force to eject the pilot and seat. The headrest (reference 5) is adjustable on the ground but the footrests (reference 10) are fixed. A safety pin (reference 3) to prevent accidental firing is connected to the right handle and is pulled when the handle is raised. An additional pin (reference 4), attached to the canopy, prevents ejection until the canopy is jettisoned. A ground safety pin (reference 13) is inserted through the channel above the trigger to prevent moving the trigger accidentally.

1-97. CONTROLS. The arm rests (reference 8) incorporate the controls to operate the ejection seat.

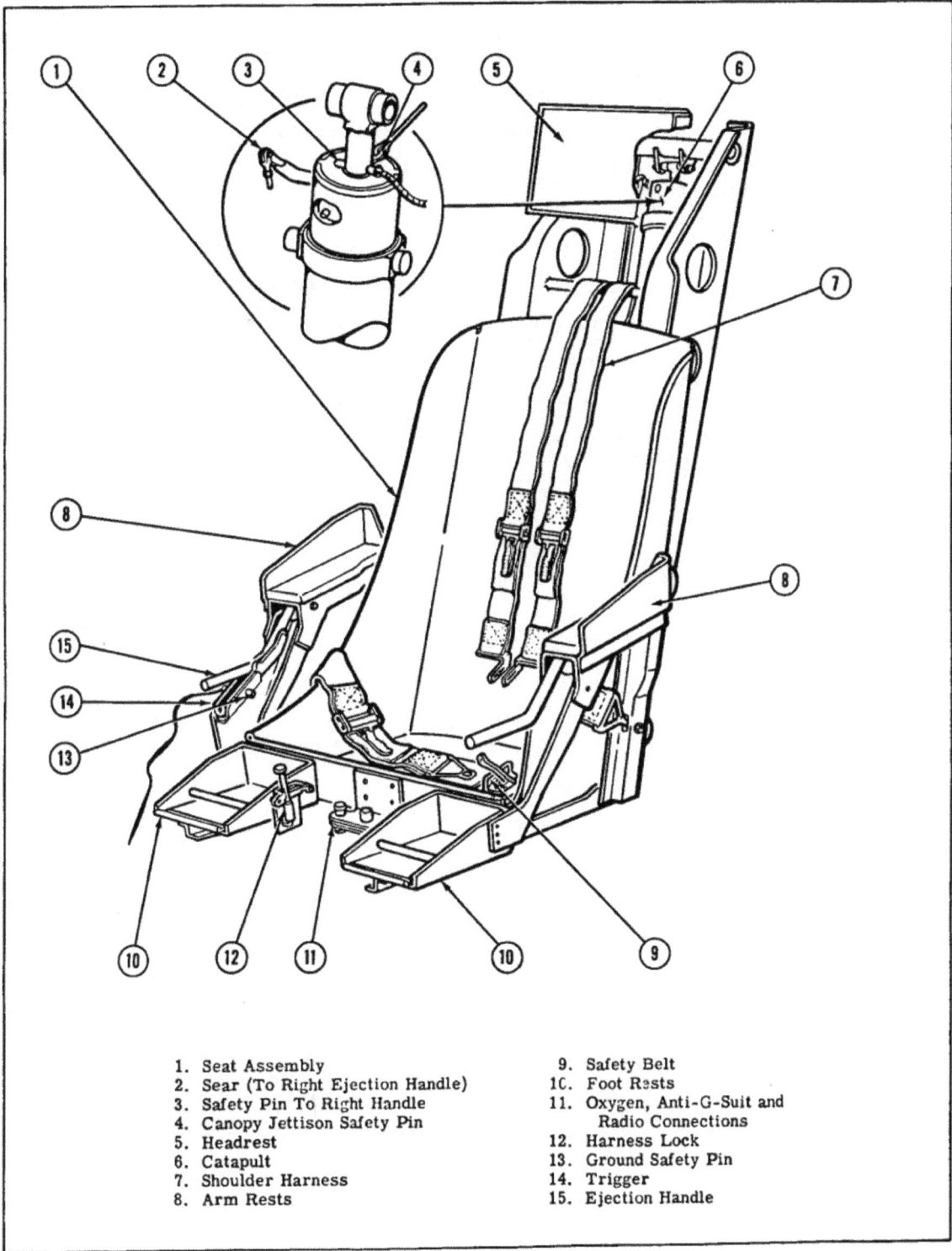

Figure 1-10. Ejection Seat

1. Seat Assembly
2. Sear (To Right Ejection Handle)
3. Safety Pin To Right Handle
4. Canopy Jettison Safety Pin
5. Headrest
6. Catapult
7. Shoulder Harness
8. Arm Rests

9. Safety Belt
10. Foot Rests
11. Oxygen, Anti-G-Suit and Radio Connections
12. Harness Lock
13. Ground Safety Pin
14. Trigger
15. Ejection Handle

The handles are safety-wired in the retracted or down position until ready for ejection. The safety wire breaks when the handles are raised and locked in the horizontal position. As the right arm rest is raised, the shoulder harness is locked, the catapult safety pin is pulled, and the trigger (reference 14) moves out of its guard to the firing position. Squeezing the trigger will fire the catapult if the canopy has been ejected. When the seat is ejected the microphone and headset connections (reference 11) and the oxygen and anti-G suit connections automatically disconnect from the fittings between the footrests.

1-98. INSTRUMENTS.

1-99. GENERAL.

1-100. The vertical gyro, directional gyro, and the turn and bank indicator operate on an a-c current supplied by an inverter connected to the aircraft's d-c system. The tachometer and tail pipe temperature circuits are self-generated, independently of the d-c or a-c circuits. The hydraulic pressure gage, the engine fuel pressure gage and the oil pressure gage are connected to the transmitters in their respective systems and operate on a-c current. The machmeter,

accelerometer and airspeed indicator are pitot-static operated. The cabin altimeter registers the pressure altitude of the cabin; the other altimeter, the pressure altitude of the airplane.

1-101. MISCELLANEOUS EQUIPMENT.

1-102. DATA CASE. A data case for flight reports, maps, etc., is located on the back of the headrest of the ejection seat.

1-103. WEATHER COVERS. Covers for the engine air intake and exhaust, the canopy and the pitot tube are supplied as loose equipment.

1-104. JACK PADS AND HOISTING SLING. Jack pads and a hoisting sling to facilitate ground handling are supplied as loose equipment.

1-105. OPERATIONAL EQUIPMENT.

1-106. GENERAL. The operational equipment, covered in Section IV, includes the oxygen system, communications, radar installation, cabin pressurization and air conditioning, and anti-G suit system.

SECTION II

NORMAL OPERATING

INSTRUCTIONS

NOTE

Sufficient space has been provided after each paragraph in this section for pilot's notes on aircraft performance or operation.

2-1. **BEFORE ENTERING CABIN.**

2-2. **RESTRICTIONS.**

Do not fly without instrumentation unless equivalent fixed ballast is installed.

Do not adjust sweep above Mach number .8.

Adjust sweep and position only in level flight.

Do not exceed 588 knots at sea level.

Do not exceed 100% rpm.

Do not exceed 715°C tail pipe temperature except during start.

Do not attempt take-off except at 20 degree sweepback.

Maximum gross weight for flight is 9893 lbs.

These limitations and restrictions are subject to change and latest service directives and orders must be consulted.

2-3. **TAKE-OFF GROSS WEIGHT AND BALANCE.**

a. Check take-off and anticipated landing gross weight and balance. (Refer to Handbook of Weight and Balance, AN 01-1B-40.)

2-4. **EXTERIOR CHECK.**

a. Check Forms F and 1 for status of airplane.

b. Check that fuel, oil, hydraulic, pneumatic, fire extinguisher and oxygen systems are serviced for flight.

c. Check that all covers and tie-down equipment are removed.

d. Check landing gear struts for proper extension and tires for inflation and general condition. Remove ground locks.

e. Check for loose, damaged or open access doors and cowling.

f. Check control surfaces for damage, security of mounting and general condition.

g. Check wing fillets at trailing and leading edge at center section for general condition.

h. Check wheel chocks in place.

i. Open the canopy by operating the crank in the fitting on the right side of the fuselage.

j. Remove safety pin from canopy remover and ejection seat trigger and check that canopy release is connected to catapult safety pin. Check cables from trigger to sear, and handle to safety pin.

k. Step over the edge of the cabin into the seat. Do not step on the canopy seal.

2-5. ON ENTERING CABIN.

a. Check landing gear control lever down.

b. Check all switches, except generator switch, "OFF".

c. Adjust rudder bar for leg length, and adjust safety belt and shoulder harness.

d. Remove gust lock, cycle the stick and check control response; check rudder response.

e. External power connected to both receptacles.

f. "CABIN AIR TEMPERATURE CONTROL" switch "AUTO".

g. Check operation of horizontal stabilizer and aileron trim tab; check visually for proper response. Return stabilizer to take-off setting and aileron to neutral.

h. Check operation of slats, return switch to "CLOSED".

i. Check operation of flaps, return switch to "UP".

j. Drag brake control lever "CLOSED".

k. Check fire detection system.

l. Check emergency landing gear air pressure.

m. Check oxygen pressure.

n. Check fuel quantity indicator reading.

o. Set clock, altimeters and accelerometer.

p. Cage flight instruments; turn "INVERTER" switch "ON".

q. Connect microphone and headset cordages, oxygen tube and anti-G suit tube.

r. Check operation of communications equipment.

s. Oxygen regulator "NORMAL".

2-6. FUEL SYSTEM MANAGEMENT.

2-7. START AND WARM-UP.

a. Start and warm up with fuel "SELECT" switch "START"-"NORMAL", "EMERG CHECK" switch "NORMAL", both "FUEL PUMP" switches "ON" and "FUEL SHUT-OFF" switch "ON".

2-8. TAKE-OFF, CLIMB AND LAND.

a. Take-off and land with "SELECT" switch "T.O. & LAND" and both pump switches "ON".

NOTE

In this configuration, the emergency fuel system is in a stand-by condition. If fuel pressure drops, the emergency fuel by-pass valve is actuated, and the amber warning light lights.

b. Climb to safe altitude and move "SELECT" switch "START-NORMAL".

2-9. CRUISE.

a. Cruise with "SELECT" switch "START-NORMAL" and both pump switches "ON".

2-10. LANDING.

a. Land with "SELECT" switch "T.O. & LAND" and both pump switches "ON".

2-11. STARTING ENGINE.

a. Purge drip pan area before each start (see figure 2-1).

b. Battery switch "OFF", external power to both receptacles.

WARNING

Use a blast deflector when starting the engine in congested areas. The tail pipe blast at 100% rpm reaches 105 knots and 60°C (140°F) 75 feet aft of the tail pipe. The suction at the intake duct is sufficiently powerful to kill or seriously injure personnel (see figure 2-2).

c. Check Generator switch "ON".

d. Fuel pump switches "ON".

e. Emergency fuel check switch "NORMAL".

f. Emergency fuel selector switch "START-NORMAL".

g. Throttle "CLOSED".

h. Fuel shut-off switch "ON".

Figure 2-1. Purging Drip Pan Area

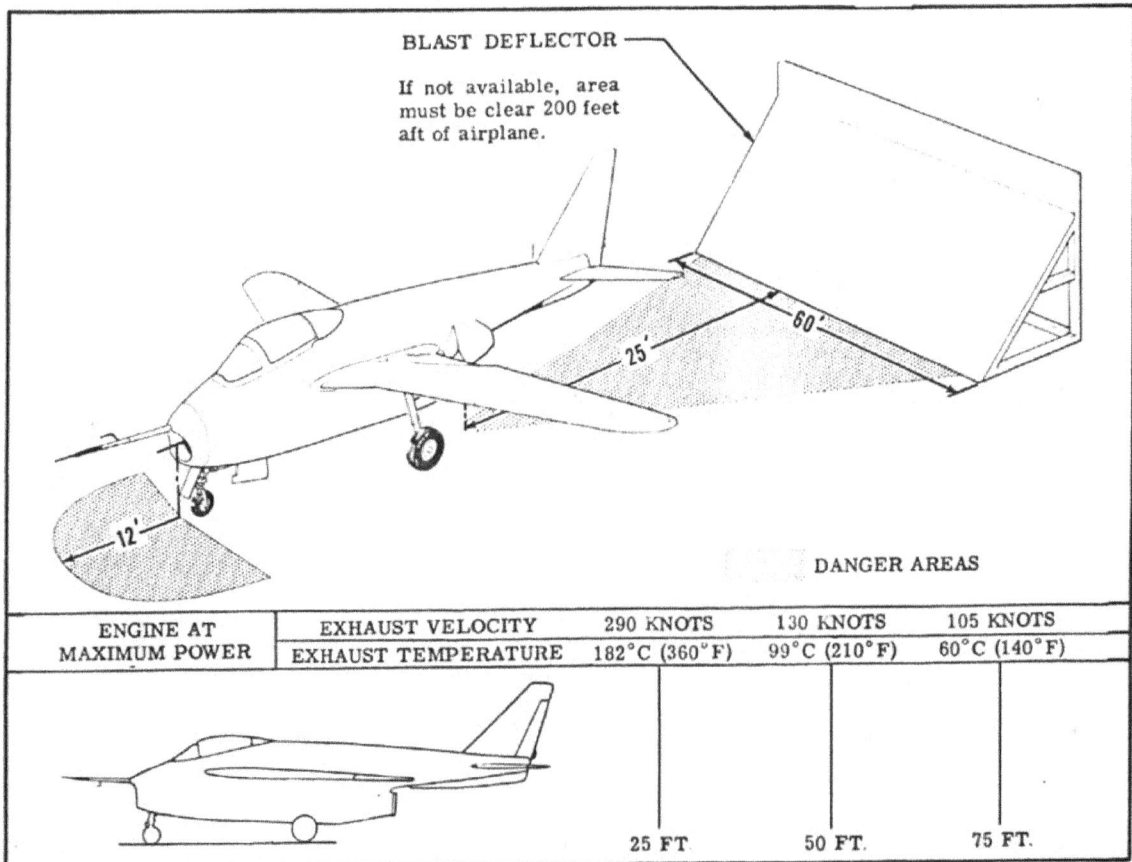

BLAST DEFLECTOR

If not available, area
must be clear 200 feet
aft of airplane.

60'

25'

12'

DANGER AREAS

ENGINE AT MAXIMUM POWER	EXHAUST VELOCITY	290 KNOTS	130 KNOTS	105 KNOTS
	EXHAUST TEMPERATURE	182°C (360°F)	99°C (210°F)	60°C (140°F)
		25 FT.	50 FT.	75 FT.

Figure 2-2. Danger Areas

i. Make sure danger areas are clear.

j. Hold starter switch "START".

NOTE

The starter will continue to crank the engine to approximately 23% rpm at which time it will automatically cut out.

k. At 7 to 9% rpm move throttle to "IDLE".

CAUTION

If 7 to 9% rpm is not reached within 40 seconds, or if combustion does not occur within three to five seconds after throttle is opened, close the throttle and move starter switch to "STOP". Hold starter switch "TEST" until engine rpm reaches 13-15% to blow unburned fuel from engine before attempting restart.

l. Adjust throttle as tail pipe temperature starts to rise to maintain temperature below 900°C until engine reaches idle rpm.

m. Close throttle and move starter switch to "STOP" if tail pipe temperature reaches 1000°C and stays there more than three seconds.

WARNING

After any five hot starts, regardless of time lapse between starts, the engine must be inspected. A hot start is one in which the tail pipe temperature exceeds 1000°C (1832°F) for 10 seconds or exceeds 900°C (1652°F) but is under 1000°C (1832°F) for 20 seconds. Enter all temperature and over speeding (in excess of 100% rpm) in Form 1. Overspeeding in excess of 4% rpm at any temperature, or 1 1/2% rpm at the above temperatures, is cause for removing the engine.

n. Check tail pipe temperature, fuel pressure and oil pressure at idle speed of approximately 35% rpm (see figure A-2).

o. External power disconnected; battery switch "ON".

2-12. WARM-UP AND GROUND TEST.

2-13. WARM-UP.

NOTE

No warm-up period is required. If instrument readings are normal and 100% rpm can be obtained, take-off may be made.

2-14. GROUND TEST.

a. Operate drag brakes through one complete cycle; observe hydraulic pressure gage and indicator lights.

b. Operate flaps, slats, aileron trim tab and stabilizer through one complete cycle at 45% to 50% rpm; observe indicators, ammeter and voltmeter.

c. Check fire detection system and indicator lights.

2-15. TAXIING.

2-16. Taxi at 50 to 55% rpm and obtain some forward motion before attempting to turn. Control heading of the airplane by brake application.

NOTE

Keep taxi time to a minimum. Fuel consumption at 50 to 55% rpm is approximately three to four gpm.

2-17. BEFORE TAKE-OFF.

2-18. After taxiing to take-off position:

a. Tighten safety belt and lock shoulder harness.

b. Slat switch "OPEN".

c. Flap switch "TAKE-OFF".

d. Check emergency fuel system, selector switch "START-NORMAL". Increase rpm to 100%, emergency check switch "EMERG CHECK" (green light is on, fuel pressure drops, amber light lights as emergency fuel system cuts in; red light stays on). Retard throttle to 75% rpm and release "EMERG CHECK" switch. (Green and amber lights go out; red light stays on.)

e. Fuel selector switch "T.O. & LAND". (Red light goes out, green light lights.)

f. Check instrument readings for desired ranges at 100% rpm (figure A-2).

g. Aileron trim tab neutral.

h. Stabilizer, take-off setting.

i. Wing sweep pointer, 20 degrees - 27 inches.

j. Position selector knob "0"; press button.

k. Check sweepback and position indicators.

l. Close canopy.

m. Uncage flight instruments.

2-19. TAKE-OFF.

NOTE

Approximate distance to clear 50-foot obstacle at normal gross weight (8980 lbs.); 20 degree sweepback and open slats is 2266 feet. At maximum gross weight (9893 lbs.) distance is 3029 feet on smooth hard runway.

a. Gradually open throttle to 100% rpm, release brakes and start take-off run.

b. Maintain directional control by brake application until rudder becomes effective.

c. As speed increases raise the nose wheel and fly the ship off the runway.

d. Raise landing gear and flaps and close slats after airborne.

e. Adjust stabilizer as necessary.

f. Fuel "SELECT" switch "START-NORMAL".

2-20. CLIMB AND LEVEL FLIGHT.

a. Estimated best rate of climb at 100% rpm, at normal gross weight and 20 degree sweepback at sea level, is 12,210 feet per minute at 377 knots.

2-21. LEVEL FLIGHT.

a. Maximum speed at 100% rpm at normal gross weight at sea level is 588 knots.

b. Use drag brakes with caution to decelerate.

2-22. NIGHT FLYING.

Not applicable.

2-23. STALLS.

2-24. Stalling speed with 56-degree flaps, slats open, 20 degree sweepback and 60 gallons of fuel is 95 knots.

2-25. SPINS.

2-26. DIVES.

2-27. APPROACH AND LANDING.

2-28. Estimated landing distance over a 50-foot obstacle with 56 degree flaps, slats open, 20 degree sweepback and 60 gallons of fuel is 2346 feet.

a. Set wing position selector knot "0".

b. Set sweepback selector 20 degrees 27 inches.

c. Press button on control stick and check indicators.

d. Fuel "SELECT" switch "T.O. & LAND".

e. Below 200 knots slat switch "OPEN". Check indicator.

f. Below 175 knots flap switch "LAND". Check indicator.

g. Below 175 knots landing gear lever down. Check indicators.

h. Make final approach at approximately 125 knots.

| WARNING |

Rapid increase in thrust is available only above approximately 60% rpm. Maintain power to have thrust available in the event of a wave-off or go-around.

i. Land in a nose high attitude at 95-100 knots.

j. Ease nose wheel down and apply brakes as necessary.

| CAUTION |

Do not apply brakes until after nose wheel has made ground contact.

k. Raise flaps and close slats before taxiing in.

2-29. STOPPING THE ENGINE.

a. Idle the engine between 35 and 50% rpm to stabilize engine speed.

b. Pull throttle past "IDLE" stop to "~~CLOSED~~". *"CUT-OFF".*

c. Turn off all switches except generator switch.

2-30. BEFORE LEAVING AIRPLANE.

a. Check landing gear lever down.

b. Check all switches "OFF" except generator switch.

c. Install safety pin in canopy remover catapult and trigger guard.

d. Complete Forms 1 and 1A.

e. Close canopy.

f. Chock wheels.

g. Install covers if airplane is not hangared.

PILOT'S NOTES

SECTION III

EMERGENCY OPERATING

INSTRUCTIONS

3-1. FIRE.

3-2. FIRE WHEN STARTING ENGINE.

3-3. If either or both warning lights come on:

a. Throttle "CLOSED".

b. "FUEL SHUT-OFF" switch "OFF".

c. Check battery switch "OFF".

d. Generator switch "OFF".

e. Actuate "DISCHARGE" switch if ground portable extinguishers are not available.

3-4. FIRE DURING FLIGHT.

3-5. If right warning light comes on during high power operation:

a. Reduce power to see if light goes off.

b. Continue flight at reduced power if light goes off.

c. Land as soon as possible.

d. Throttle "CLOSED" if light stays on.

e. "FUEL SHUT-OFF" switch "OFF".

f. Actuate "DISCHARGE" switch.

g. If left warning light comes on, assume there is a fire and actuate the discharge switch.

WARNING

If lights stay on after extinguisher discharge and the presence of fire is assured, or a dead stick landing is impossible, abandon the aircraft (refer to paragraph 3-10).

3-6. ENGINE FAILURE.

3-7. DURING TAKE-OFF RUN.

a. Throttle "CLOSED".

b. Fuel shut-off, battery and generator switches "OFF".

c. Apply brakes.

NOTE

If crash is inevitable, just prior to impact, turn battery switch "ON", actuate fire extinguisher "DISCHARGE" switch and turn battery switch "OFF".

3-8. AFTER LEAVING GROUND.

a. Throttle "CLOSED".

b. Fuel shut-off and generator switches "OFF".

c. Landing gear control lever "UP" if terrain will not permit a wheel landing.

d. Land straight ahead.

NOTE

If full power failure occurs on take-off, there will be a large change in longitudinal trim towards nose-down, and will require a quick and vigorous stick movement to correct.

e. Flap switch "LAND".

f. Jettison the canopy (refer to paragraph 3-11b and c). Lock shoulder harness.

g. Actuate fire extinguisher "DISCHARGE" switch and turn battery switch "OFF" just prior to ground contact.

3-9. DURING FLIGHT.

WARNING

Close throttle as soon as flame-out occurs to prevent flooding the engine and tail pipe with fuel. Flame-out is usually caused by too rapid movement of the throttle, or low fuel pressure at altitude.

a. Throttle "CLOSED".

b. Glide down below 20,000 feet, keep air speed high to maintain a windmill speed of 19 to 26% rpm.

c. Fuel selector switch "START-NORMAL".

d. Pull up sharply to drain fuel from tail pipe.

e. Test switch "IGNITION TEST".

f. Open throttle half way.

23

3-14. ELECTRICAL FAILURE.   3-17. CABIN PRESSURIZATION OR AIR CONDITIONING FAILURE.

Section III
Paragraph 3-10 to 3-19
RESTRICTED

g. Manipulate throttle to maintain rpm and temperatures within limits when combustion occurs.

> **WARNING**
>
> If tail pipe temperature reaches 1000°C and stays there for more than three seconds, close throttle immediately and attempt a restart.

3-10. EMERGENCY EXIT.

3-11. In all cases of bail-out, clear the ship by means of seat ejection (see figure 3-1).

a. Pull ball handle on bail-out bottle if at altitude.

b. Release shoulder harness lock and bend head and body as low as possible.

c. Pull canopy jettison handle.

d. Disconnect oxygen hose, anti-G connection and microphone cordage.

NOTE

If immediate abandonment is necessary, omit step d. The equipment will be automatically disconnected at ejection.

e. Place feet in footrests, sit erect with head against headrest, and chin tucked in.

f. Raise both handles until they lock.

NOTE

As right handle is raised, the shoulder harness is locked, the catapult safety pin is pulled and the firing trigger is brought into position.

g. Squeeze trigger.

h. Release harness and safety belt and kick free of seat.

i. Delay opening parachute as long as possible to insure seat will not foul chute and to reduce shock when chute opens.

3-12. LANDING GEAR EMERGENCY OPERATION.

3-13. In the event of hydraulic system failure, the landing gear may be extended by using the emergency pneumatic system.

a. Move landing gear handle to "DOWN" and allow gear to fall free.

b. Operate emergency landing gear control valve by pressing the emergency release button and moving the landing gear control lever full down.

c. Check wheel position indicators and warning light.

NOTE

Drag brakes will be inoperative if hydraulic system fails.

3-14. ELECTRICAL FAILURE.

3-15. COMPLETE FAILURE. In the event of complete electrical failure, some of the controls and much of the equipment will be inoperative. The flaps, slats, wing sweep and position, aileron and stabilizer trim will be inoperative. However, the stabilizer may be trimmed with the manual override trim wheel (figure 1-2, reference 20) and the wing sweep and position may be operated with the hand crank (figure 1-3, reference 19). The inverter, gyro instruments and fuel booster pumps will also be inoperative. Continue flight as follows:

a. Reduce power and altitude to maintain satisfactory engine operation.

b. Turn off all electrical equipment.

c. Land approximately 25 to 45 knots above normal stalling speed.

3-16. GENERATOR FAILURE. If generator fails, but battery power is still available:

a. Turn off all unnecessary electrical equipment.

b. Reduce power and altitude for contact flight.

c. Use battery power sparingly to have sufficient power available for slat and flap extension when making landing approach.

3-17. CABIN PRESSURIZATION OR AIR CONDITIONING FAILURE.

3-18. PRESSURIZATION FAILURE. If the cabin pressure regulator fails or the pressure line is damaged:

a. Move the "CABIN PRESSURE DUMP VALVE" control lever (figure 1-2, reference 3) above the left console aft to open airscoop and cabin pressure dump valve and shut-off air conditioning.

b. Set oxygen regulator to aircraft altitude.

c. Descend to a safe altitude.

3-19. AIR CONDITIONING FAILURE. If the cabin temperature control fails, and the temperature cannot be controlled by the "CABIN TEMPERATURE CONTROL" switch.

a. Move switch to "OFF".

b. Move "CABIN PRESSURE DUMP VALVE" control lever aft.

c. Set oxygen regulator to aircraft altitude.

d. Control temperature by moving lever fore and aft.

1

At altitude pull ball
handle on bail-out bottle.

2

Release shoulder harness,
bend forward, keep head
and body as low as possible
and pull "CANOPY JETTISON"
handle.

3

Sit erect with head
hard back against
headrest and chin
tucked in. Brace arms
on armrests and pull
up handles.

6

Delay opening parachute as
long as altitude will permit
to allow seat to clear parachute canopy and reduce
parachute opening shock.

5

After seat has been ejected,
release safety harness and
kick away from seat as soon
as possible.

4

Squeeze trigger

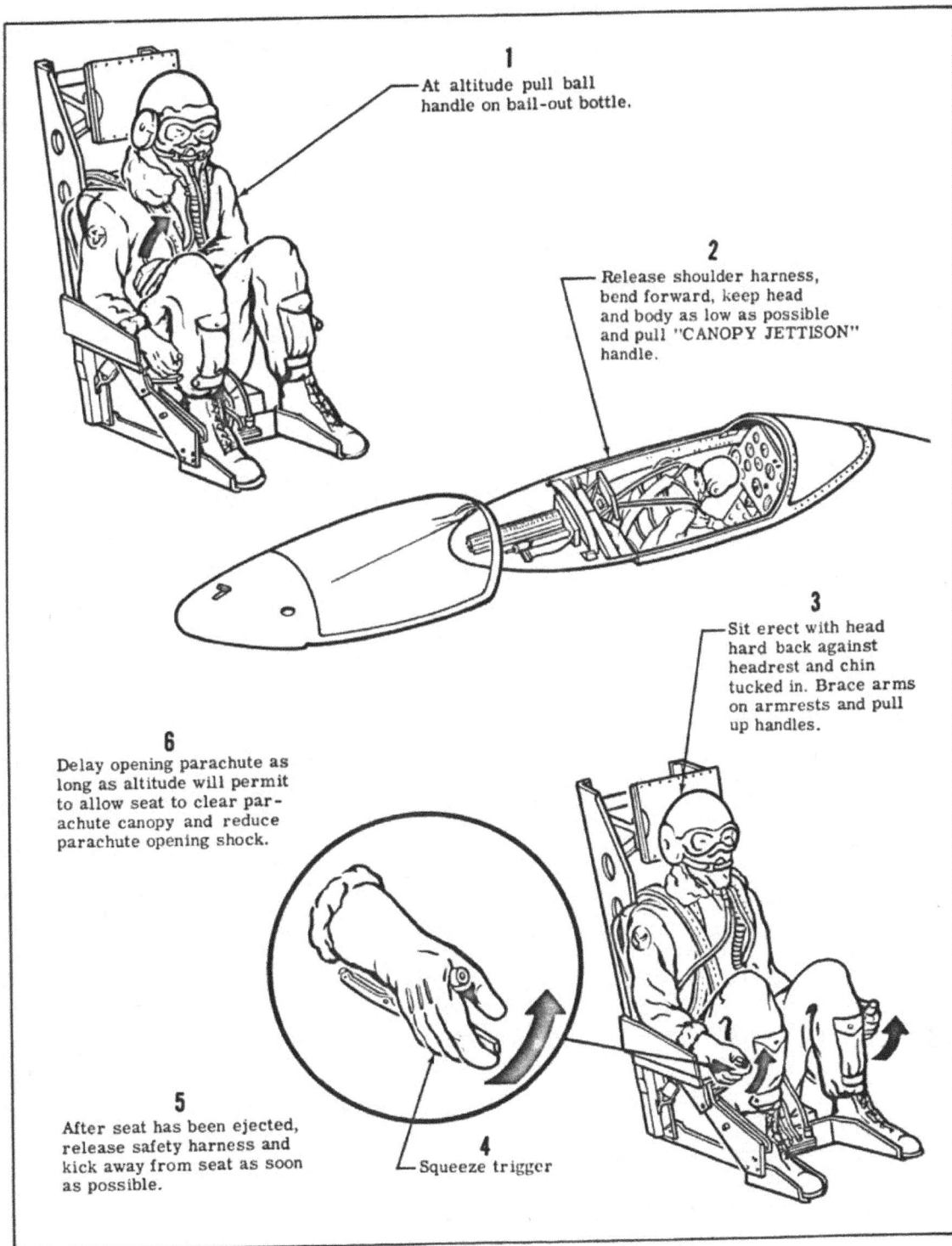

Figure 3-1. Seat Ejection Procedures

PILOT'S NOTES

SECTION IV

OPERATIONAL EQUIPMENT

4-1. OXYGEN SYSTEM.

4-2. GENERAL.

4-3. The low pressure oxygen system consists of two type D-2 cylinders mounted under the cabin floor, which are serviced through the filler valve at the side of the airplane, a flow indicator and a pressure gage. (Figure 4-1.)

4-4. OXYGEN SYSTEM CONTROLS. With the regulator (figure 1-4, reference 24) set at "NORMAL OXYGEN", flow is regulated by the pilot's needs; with the regulator at "100% OXYGEN", no dilution occurs and pure oxygen is supplied. The supply is depleted much more rapidly with the regulator at "100% OXYGEN". (See figure 4-2.)

4-5. OXYGEN SYSTEM INDICATORS. The pressure gage (figure 1-4, reference 19) denotes system pressure; normal full pressure is 450 psi. The flow indicator (blinker) (reference 23) shows when oxygen is being consumed.

NOTE

Use oxygen with reference to the cabin altimeter.

4-6. COMMUNICATIONS EQUIPMENT.

4-7. GENERAL.

4-8. The communications equipment is a VHF command set AN/ARC-5, consisting of an R-28/ARC-5 receiver, a T-23/ARC-5 transmitter, an MD-7/ARC-5 modulator, a headset and microphone.

4-9. COMMUNICATIONS CONTROLS. The "CHANNEL SELECT" switch on the right console selects any one of the four channels "A", "B", "C" or "D". The control knob (figure 1-3, reference 7), marked "VOLUME", controls the audio strength of the signal. The "RADIO" switch (reference 8) turns the set "ON" or "OFF". The button on the top of the throttle (figure 1-2, reference 7) is held down to transmit.

4-10. RADAR INSTALLATION.

4-11. GENERAL.

4-12. The AN/APN-60 radar beacon consists of a RT-126/APN-60 receiver-transmitter, a DY-56/APN-60 dynamotor unit, a F-28/APN-19 filter and the transmitter and receiver antennas. The set receives signals from an interrogating ground station within the range of 2700 to 2900 megacycles. When inter-

rogated, the set transmits a signal preset within the range of 2800 to 2920 megacycles to the interrogating station, enabling the ground station to establish the range and azimuth of the airplane, up to 50,000 feet in the radar line of sight, to approximately 150 miles.

4-13. RADAR CONTROLS. The beacon is turned "ON" or "OFF" by the "RADAR BEACON" switch (figure 1-3, reference 9) on the right console.

4-14. CABIN PRESSURIZATION AND AIR CONDITIONING.

4-15. PRESSURIZATION.

4-16. The cabin is pressurized through the air conditioning system, and the differential pressure is maintained by the pressure regulator on the right console.

4-17. AIR CONDITIONING.

4-18. Cabin air temperature control is accomplished through an air bleed from the engine compressor. The air passes through a pressure control valve, a shut-off valve, a flow control valve, a refrigeration unit and modulating by-pass valve, and ducts to the outlet valve in the floor ahead of the seat and to the windshield defroster outlet. The modulating valve mixes the air to the ducts in proportions set by the "CABIN TEMPERATURE CONTROL" on the left console. (See figure 4-3.) An emergency system, which closes the shut-off valve, opens the cabin dump valve and an air scoop on the left side of the fuselage, is operated by the lever above the left console (figure 1-2, reference 3).

4-19. CABIN PRESSURIZATION AND AIR CONDITIONING CONTROLS.

4-20. The "CABIN TEMPERATURE CONTROL" switch (figure 1-2, reference 22), through temperature control unit causes the modulating by-pass valve to raise or lower cabin temperature when the switch is in "AUTO", and the knob (reference 21) adjacent to the switch is rotated. When the switch is moved to "HOT" or "COLD", it overrides the automatic temperature control. When the switch is moved to "OFF", the system is inoperative.

4-21. EMERGENCY AIR CONTROL. When the "CABIN PRESSURE DUMP VALVE" control lever above the left console (figure 1-2, reference 3) is moved aft, the ram air scoop on the left side of fuselage is opened to admit rammed air to the cockpit. Linkage connected to the lever opens the cabin pressure dump valve and actuates a microswitch which shuts off the shut-off valve in the compressor bleed. When the control lever is forward, normal cabin pressurization and air-conditioning are established.

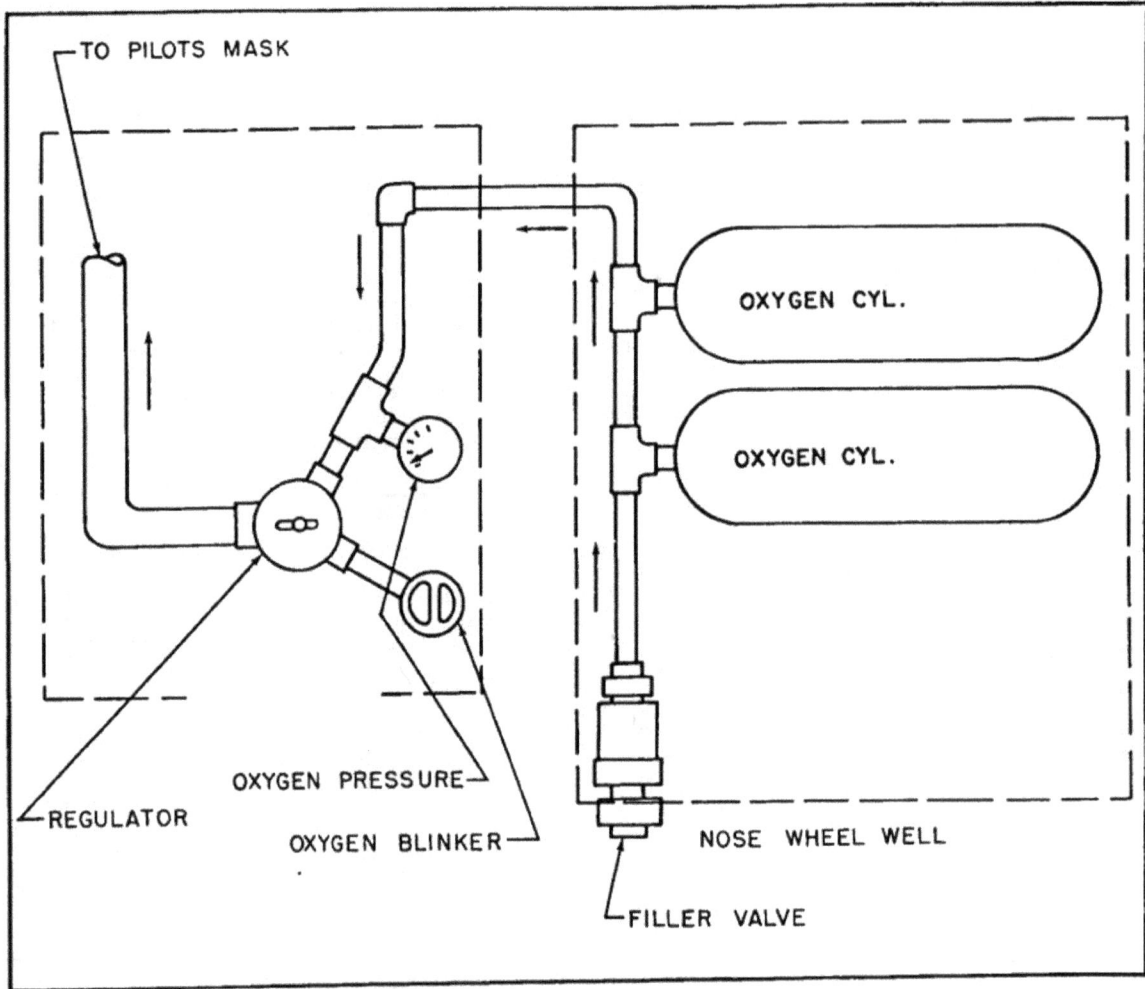

Figure 4-1. Oxygen System Diagram

			GAGE PRESSURE - PSI					
CABIN ALT. FEET								BELOW
	400	350	300	250	200	150	100	
40,000	3.8	3.3	2.7	2.2	1.6	1.1	0.5	Descend below 10,000 Feet Altitude
35,000	2.8	2.4	2.	1.6	1.2	0.8	0.4	
30,000	2.1	1.8	1.5	1.2	0.9	0.6	0.3	
25,000	2.0	1.7	1.4	1.1	0.8	0.5	0.3	
20,000	2.2	1.9	1.6	1.3	0.9	0.6	0.3	
15,000	2.7	2.3	1.9	1.5	1.1	1.2	0.4	
10,000	3.6	3.1	2.6	2.0	1.5	1.0	0.5	
APPROXIMATE DURATION - REGULATOR "NORMAL"								

Figure 4-2. Man-Hour Oxygen Consumption Chart

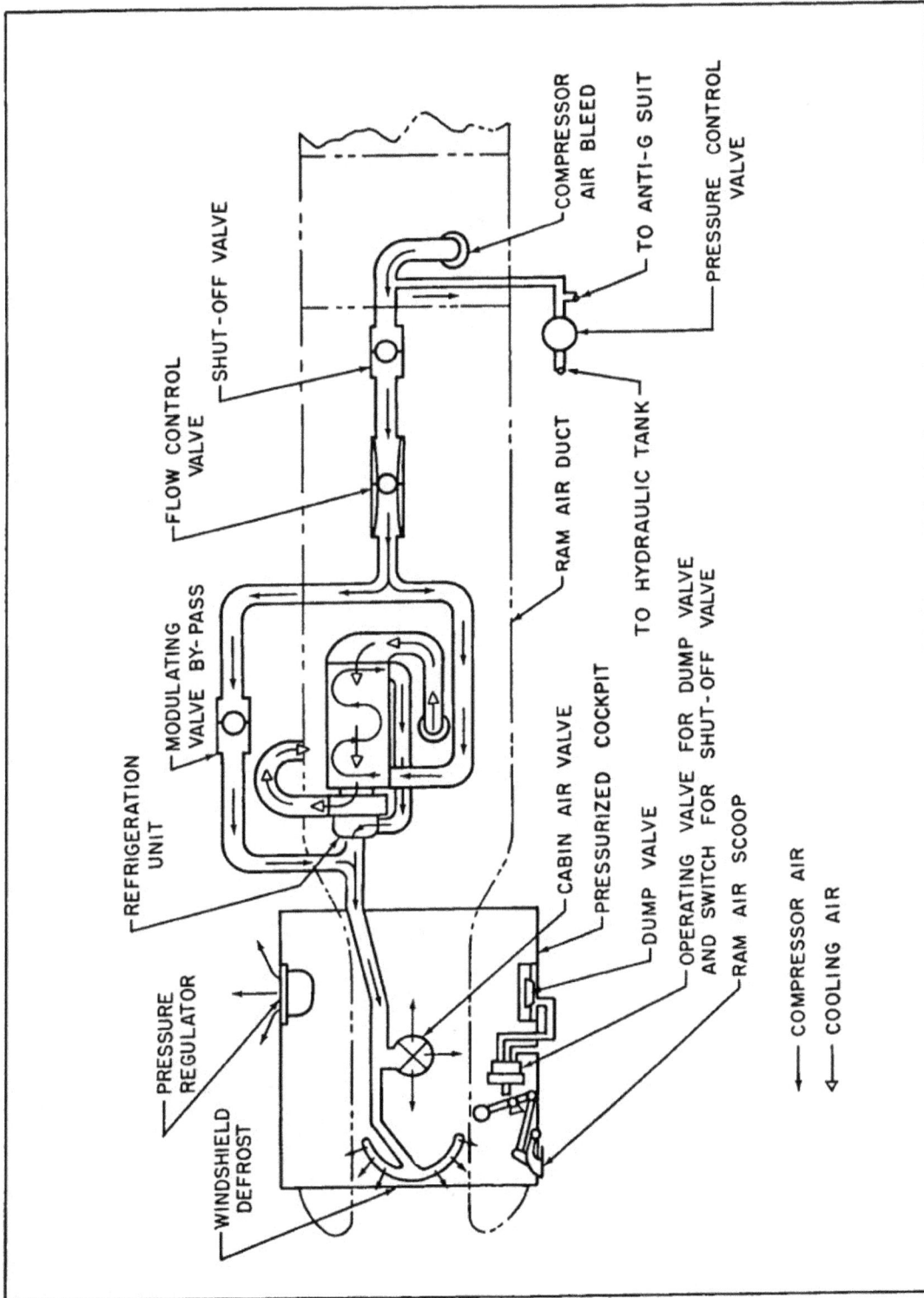

Figure 4-3. Cabin Pressurization and Airconditioning Diagram

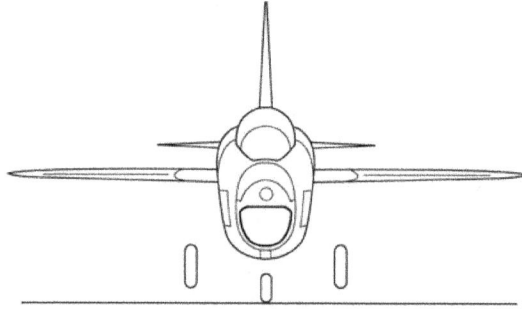

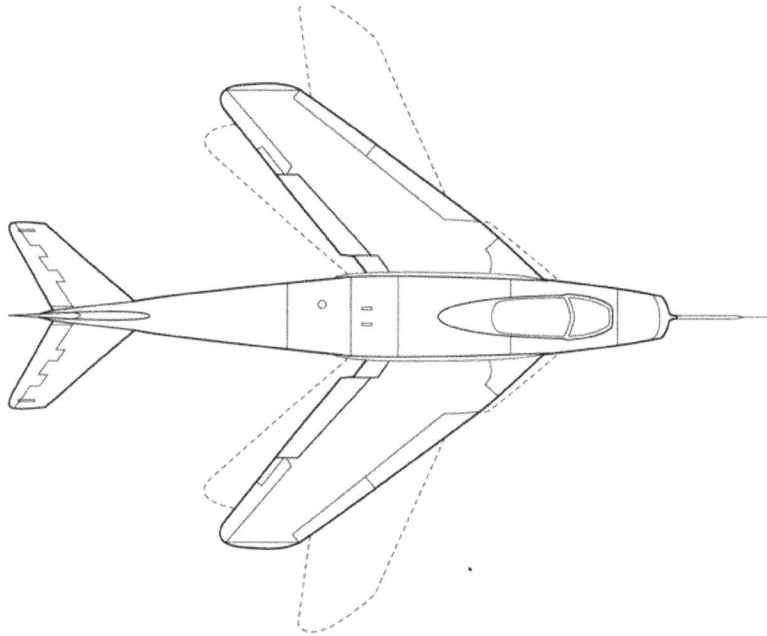

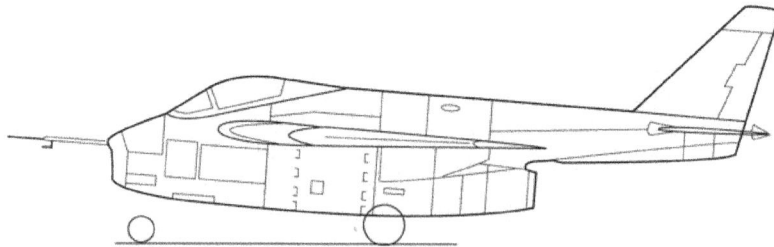

APPENDIX I

OPERATIONAL DATA

I. A. S.   CORRECTED I. A. S.   —

Figure A-1. Airspeed Correction Table

To be filled out by the pilot when information is available.

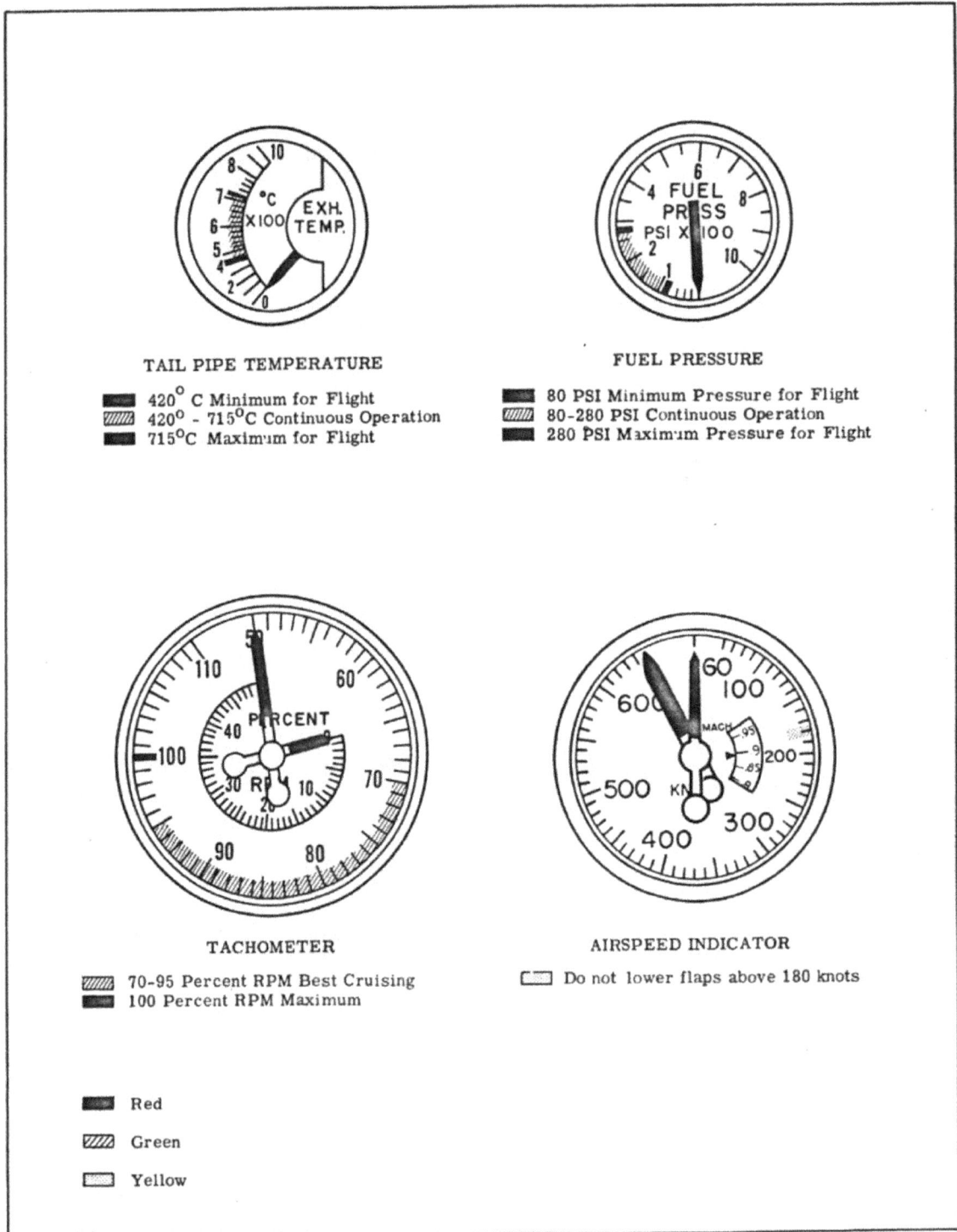

TAIL PIPE TEMPERATURE

420° C Minimum for Flight
420° - 715°C Continuous Operation
715°C Maximum for Flight

FUEL PRESSURE

80 PSI Minimum Pressure for Flight
80-280 PSI Continuous Operation
280 PSI Maximum Pressure for Flight

TACHOMETER

70-95 Percent RPM Best Cruising
100 Percent RPM Maximum

AIRSPEED INDICATOR

Do not lower flaps above 180 knots

Red

Green

Yellow

Figure A-2. Instrument Markings Diagram (Sheet 1 of 2 Sheets)

OIL PRESSURE

■■■ 10 PSI Minimum Pressure for Flight
▨▨▨ 10-55 PSI Continuous Operation
■■■ 55 PSI Maximum Pressure for Flight

HYDRAULIC PRESSURE

■■■ 2700 PSI Minimum Operating Pressure
▨▨▨ 2700 - 3000 PSI Continuous Operation
■■■ 3500 PSI Maximum Operating Pressure

LANDING GEAR
EMERGENCY PRESSURE

■■■ 2300 PSI Minimum Operating Pressure
▨▨▨ 2300 - 2400 PSI Normal Operating Pressure
■■■ 2400 PSI Maximum Operating Pressure

■■■ Red

▨▨▨ Green

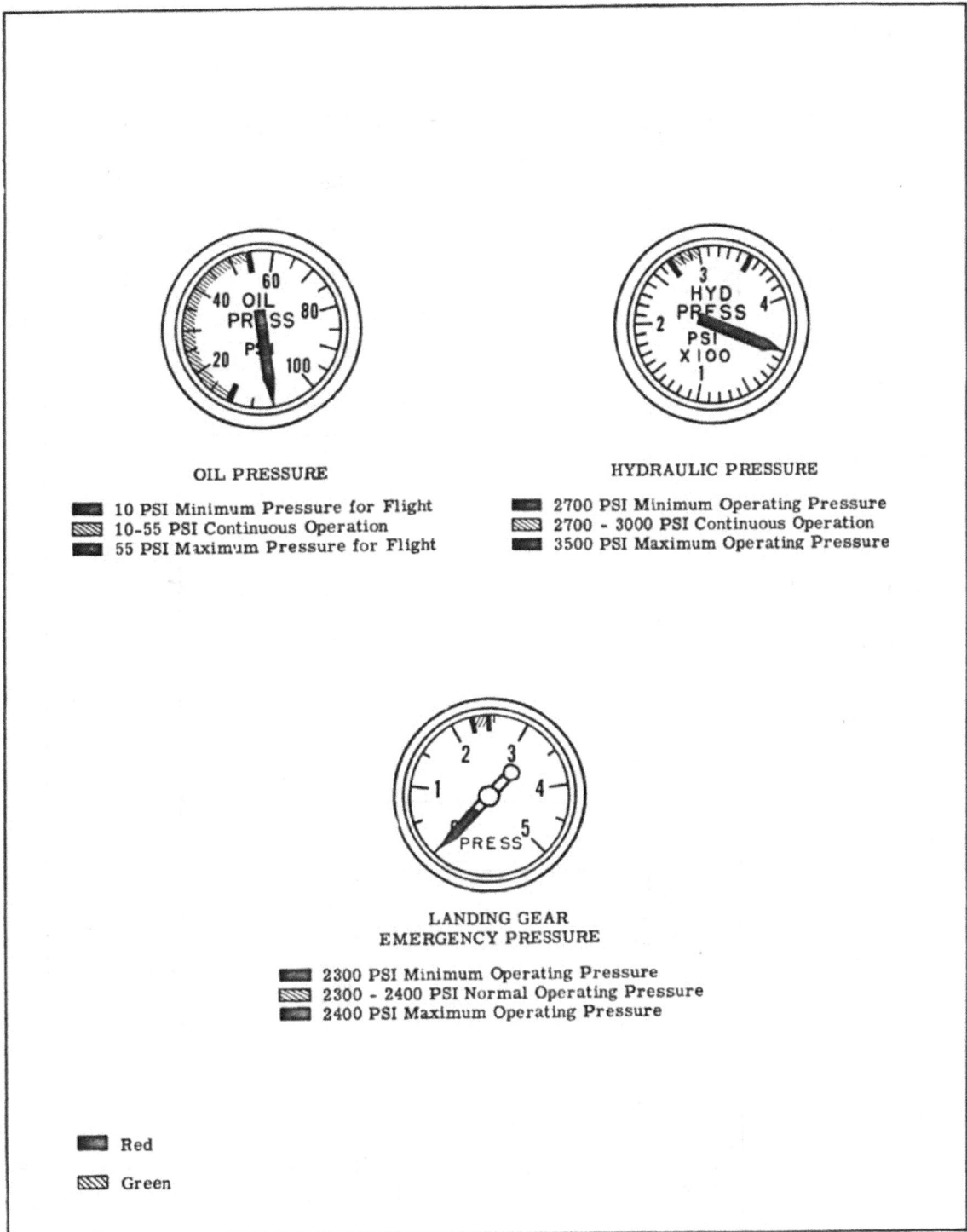

Figure A-2. Instrument Markings Diagram (Sheet 2 of 2 Sheets)

NCRE Form No. 239C (5 May 48)

AIRPLANE MODEL(S)

ENGINE(S):

FLIGHT OPERATION INSTRUCTION CHART

CHART WEIGHT LIMITS TO POUNDS

EXTERNAL LOAD ITEMS

NUMBER OF ENGINES OPERATING:

LIMITS	TIME LIMIT	% RPM	TAIL PIPE TEMP. °C	OIL PRESS PSI		
MILITARY						
NORMAL						

INSTRUCTIONS FOR USING CHART: (A) IN FLIGHT-Select figure in fuel column equal to or less than fuel on board. Move horizontally right or left to section according to present altitude and read total range available (no wind) by cruising at that altitude or by climbing to another altitude for maximum range. For a flight at initial altitude, operating instructions are given directly below. For a flight at higher altitude, climb immediately to desired altitude and read cruising instructions in appropriate cruising altitude section. (B) FLIGHT PLANNING-Subtract fuel required for take-off and climb to altitude. Then use chart as for IN FLIGHT above, adding initial climb distance to range values.

NOTES: Ranges shown at optimum altitudes are maximum. In order to obtain maximum range on flights requiring more than one chart (due to external configuration or gross weight change), it is necessary to observe the optimum cruising altitude on each chart: i.e., when changing charts a climb may be required to obtain maximum range. All range values include allowances for descent distance and fuel plus reserve shown for landing. Climb distance and fuel are included where climbs are indicated.

IF YOU ARE AT			IF YOU ARE AT			FUEL U.S. GAL.	IF YOU ARE AT			IF YOU ARE AT			FUEL U.S. GAL.	IF YOU ARE AT			IF YOU ARE AT		
RANGE IN AIRMILES			RANGE IN AIRMILES				RANGE IN AIRMILES			RANGE IN AIRMILES				RANGE IN AIRMILES			RANGE IN AIRMILES		
BY CRUISING AT	OPT. ALT.	BY CRUISING AT OPT. ALT.	BY CRUISING AT	OPT. ALT.	BY CRUISING AT OPT. ALT.		BY CRUISING AT	OPT. ALT.	BY CRUISING AT OPT. ALT.	BY CRUISING AT	OPT. ALT.	BY CRUISING AT OPT. ALT.		BY CRUISING AT	OPT. ALT.	BY CRUISING AT OPT. ALT.	BY CRUISING AT	OPT. ALT.	BY CRUISING AT OPT. ALT.
(RANGE FIGURES INCLUDE ALLOWANCES FOR PRESCRIBED CLIMB, DESCENT TO SEA LEVEL AND GALLON LANDING RESERVE)																			

CRUISING AT						CRUISING AT						EFFEC-TIVE WIND	CRUISING AT						CRUISING AT						EFFEC-TIVE WIND	CRUISING AT						CRUISING AT					
RANGE FACTOR	% RPM	LET-DOWN DIST.	APPROXIMATE			RANGE FACTOR	% RPM	LET-DOWN DIST.	APPROXIMATE				RANGE FACTOR	% RPM	LET-DOWN DIST.	APPROXIMATE			RANGE FACTOR	% RPM	LET-DOWN DIST.	APPROXIMATE				RANGE FACTOR	% RPM	LET-DOWN DIST.	APPROXIMATE			RANGE FACTOR	% RPM	LET-DOWN DIST.	APPROXIMATE		
			CAS	GPH	GS.				CAS	GPH	GS.					CAS	GPH	GS.				CAS	GPH	GS.					CAS	GPH	GS.				CAS	GPH	GS.
												120 HW													120 HW												
												80 HW													80 HW												
												40 HW													40 HW												
												0													0												
												40 TW													40 TW												
												80 TW													80 TW												
												120 TW													120 TW												

SPECIAL NOTES

(1) MULTIPLY STATUTE UNITS BY .87 FOR CONVERSION TO NAUTICAL UNITS

EXAMPLE

LEGEND

EFFECTIVE WIND – HW. HEADWIND, TW. TAILWIND

RANGE FACTOR – RATIO OF GROUND DISTANCE TO AIR-MILES FOR CORRESPONDING WINDS

G.S. – GROUND SPEED – STATUTE MILES PER HR.

CAS – CALIBRATED AIRSPEED IN STATUTE MILES PER HOUR

DATA AS OF: BASED ON:

BASED ON FUEL

RED FIGURES HAVE NOT BEEN FLIGHT CHECKED

Figure A-3. Flight Operation Instruction Chart

36

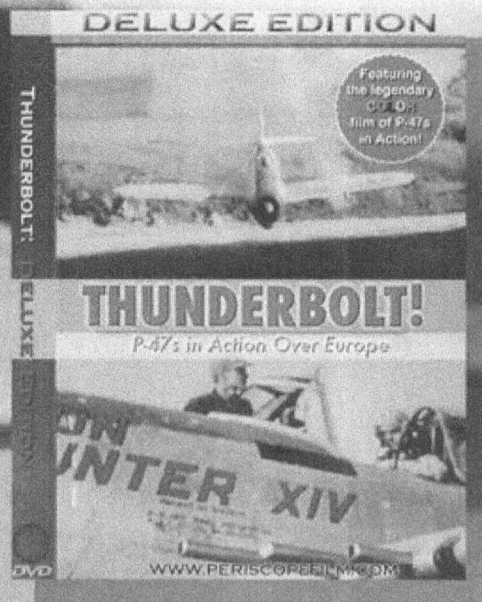

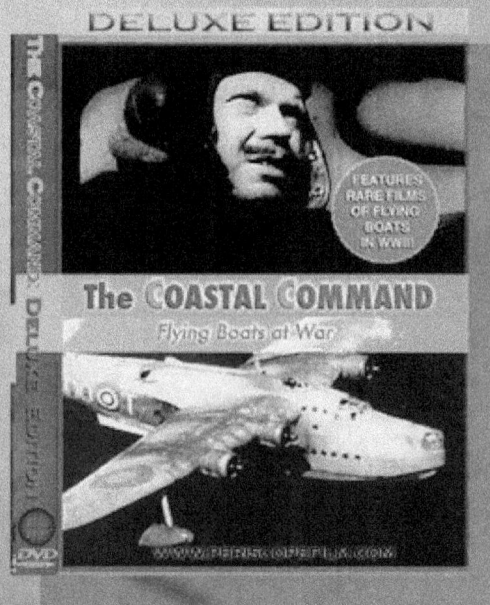

ISBN # 978-1-935327-69-1   1-935327-69-0

www.ingramcontent.com/pod-product-compliance
Lightning Source LLC
Chambersburg PA
CBHW062109090426
42741CB00015B/3370